HOW TO
MAKE WOODEN TOYS
AND GAMES

Other Books by Walter E. Schutz:

Getting Started in Candlemaking
How to Attract, House and Feed Birds

HOW TO MAKE WOODEN TOYS AND GAMES

WALTER E. SCHUTZ

COLLIER BOOKS
A Division of Macmillan Publishing Co., Inc.
New York

COLLIER MACMILLAN PUBLISHERS
London

Macmillan Publishing Co., Inc.
866 Third Avenue, New York, N.Y. 10022
Collier-Macmillan Canada Ltd.

First Printing 1975

Library of Congress Cataloging in Publication Data

Schutz, Walter E.
  How to make wooden toys and games.

  First published in 1966 under title: Toys for fun
and how to make them.

  1. Wooden toy making.   I. Title.
[TT174.5.W6S38   1975b]   745.59'2   75-1330
ISBN 0-02-081950-1

How to Make Wooden Toys and Games is also published in a hardcover edition by Macmillan Publishing Co., Inc. It was previously published by The Bruce Publishing Company under the title Toys for Fun and How to Make Them.

Printed in the United States of America

Contents

PART 2:
HOW TO MAKE WHEELS   105

SUPPLIERS   119

Foreword

You enjoy many benefits when you build your own wooden toys. Since these advantages are all interrelated, one enhances the other, and as a result your various experiences will always be pleasant, happy ones.

One of the first and most apparent benefits is that you save money. As you well know, prices of manufactured toys climb every time you go to the toy shop or toy department. By making them yourself you can, for just a dollar or two, buy enough wood for several toys. Nails, screws, glue, and finishing materials add only a little more. In other words, for the cost of one manufactured toy you can make five or six of your own.

But as gratifying as it is to be able to save money, there are some satisfactions that no amount of money can buy. You'll know what I mean when you put your first handmade toy into the hands of a child!

WALTER E. SCHUTZ
Washington Island, Wisconsin

Danke schön

My thanks to the following people at Macmillan
Publishing Co., Inc., who made this book possible: Constance Schrader, who revived interest
in the book and who realized that an up-to-date
version would provide helpful, practical assistance to anyone who wants to enjoy the satisfaction of building wooden toys compatible with
today's goals of fun and beauty combined with
safety; Lorraine Steurer, who improved the
manuscript; and Peter Jovanovich, who followed through during the book's final stages.

Introduction

Pride in Accomplishment   Everyone appreciates a compliment. The builders of homemade toys receive many. It is a great feeling when friends admire your handiwork, but perhaps the biggest and warmest compliment will come from your children when they boast: "My daddy [or mother] made this!" There will be a closer bond between you and the children because you will be giving a part of yourself. It will be an entirely new, thrilling experience for them to know that the toy was made especially for them and that it did not come out of a store where there are hundreds more just like it.

Easy and Simple to Do   At first, making a toy out of wood may seem like a complicated job. Yet if you have had any industrial art work or manual training in school, you have already been exposed to this fascinating craft of woodworking. To start, do not attempt the more complex toys. Stay with something simple, such as ordinary building blocks. They provide a great deal of fun, and stimulate the child's imagination and creativeness. Next try your hand at a simple boat. Bit by bit you will gain confidence, and in a short while you will be making more elaborate toys. You may even make a few of your own design!

Designs Are Simple to Follow   The designs in this book are for toys, playthings. They are not intended to be models. There is a vast difference between a toy and a model. Toys are for children to play with, and do not need a lot of intricate detail— the child's own imagination will supply whatever is necessary to make it the way he or she wants it to be. Children want rugged toys that will hold up under rough handling. Purchased toys often fall apart after the first day of play.

As a parent, grandparent, aunt, or uncle, how often have you found the child paying more attention to the wrapping material and the carton the toy came in than to the actual toy itself? Perhaps the toy was *too* complete. The child could add nothing of his own, whereas the box and the wrapping gave him a chance to imagine all sorts of wonderful things.

Too often a toy is so refined in detail that it reflects more the ambition of the builder than his desire to provide a toy for play. Researchers in the U. S. Office of Education have found that a long period of play is required before children develop the concentration that is required later when they are learning to read or studying math. Imaginative, creative toys such as those suggested here provide the stimulus that will make such later concentration easier.

Why Wood?   There are several simple reasons: Wood is available anywhere. It is low in cost, and the most inexperienced person can cut, form, and finish it for

1

satisfactory results. It is a good experience for your children to feel a natural product. Wood is so interesting, so pleasant to the touch. It is completely harmless, and has none of the cold, impersonal characteristics of plastics or metal. Besides, wood is completely biodegradeable, an important factor in these days of ecological concern.

The Beauty of Wood   There is no substitute for wood. No man-made material has the warmth, the natural feel, the weight, or the intimacy that a piece of wood delivers. The beauty of the grain adds immeasurably to its appearance. You find this in mahogany, walnut, cherry, oak, and the "exotic" woods that come from far-off places. Even common white pine has a character of its own. A knot, when you actually examine it, is a marvel of nature's development—no man can make anything as handsome. And wood can take such a harmless and excellent finish. Give it a coat of clear lacquer or a few coats or wax, and you preserve its natural beauty for all time. Yet, though it seems almost a pity to cover the natural grain with paint or stain, at times painting or staining must be done. Then cheaper, more common woods can be used.

MATERIALS NEEDED

One of the big advantages in building wooden toys is that all the materials needed are easily available at low cost. Wood dowels, nails, screws, glue, and finishing materials are the only things necessary and you can get them all at either your local lumberyard or hardware or department store. The easiest wood to work with at the start is pine. You can get it in thicknesses of ⅜ (drawer sides), ¾, and 1⅛ inches. Ordinary 2 x 4's, usually 1⅝ x 3⅝ inches, can also be used—but be sure these are of the softest pine, not the hard yellow pine or hemlock used in building construction. Tell your lumber dealer what you want the lumber for and he will give you the correct wood. If you have a cabinet shop or other woodworking plant in your locality, pay them a visit. They usually have piles and boxes of scrap that you can have for no other cost than hauling it away. This is kiln-dried wood, excellent for toy-building. Ask for scraps of plywood and paneling, too. Scout around and ask a lot of questions. Pattern shops associated with foundries are another source of pine and mahogany. You need so little, and it goes so far. A trunkful of scrap will build a hundred toys!

Buy your dowels, in diameters of ¼, ⅜, ½, ¾, and 1 inch, at the hardware store. Get your nails, screws, bolts, glue, and finishing materials there also.

Exotic Woods   Pine is fine for toys, but it has little or no noticeable grain. For wood with more character which becomes more prominent with a clear finish, use black walnut, butternut, chestnut, mahogany, cherry, or birch. With the exception of the mahogany, these are all native woods and, again, you may be able to pick up some of them at your local cabinet or woodworking shop. Imported woods such as avodire, bubinga, limba, purpleheart, rosewood, and zebrawood are extremely beautiful, with bold grain and color, and toys made of these become true works of art and craftsmanship. These imported products are hardwoods and are perhaps a little more difficult to cut and shape; but the end product is so pleasing and startlingly attractive that it is worth the effort. (For sources of exotic woods, see "Suppliers" at back of book.)

WORKING AREA OR SHOP

You can set aside any place you desire for your shop or working area. If possible, have it located in a place that you can step into at any time and enjoy your work, such as the basement. The garage is suitable in summer, but is usually too cold in winter, the time you will want to do most of your toy-making. Have adequate light, with one or two electrical outlets handy. Build a bench, as shown, out of ordinary pine building-construction lumber, and mount your tool-rack board on the wall above the bench.

A Suggestion: You'll do better work and get it done sooner if you complete your working area before you start making toys. With a good bench, good lighting, your tools and all other items neatly arranged and within convenient reach, you will enjoy your toy-building right from the beginning and be able to do more work in less time, for there will be no need to hunt for tools, etc.

A STURDY, INEXPENSIVE WORKBENCH

You can use an old table or some other setup for your workbench but too often these units are too low or too light and unsteady for such use. We suggest you build a bench as shown. You can get the lumber cut the correct length at your lumberyard so that all you have to do is assemble it, using No. 10 screws, 1½ inches long. Use ordinary building-construction lumber—white pine.

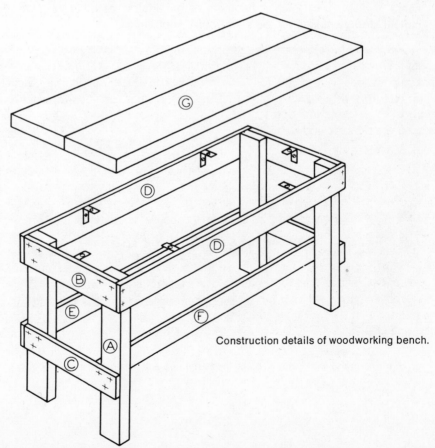

Construction details of woodworking bench.

Part	Name	No. Required	Size in Inches
A	Legs	4	2 x 4, 30 long
B	Top-End Cleats	2	1 x 8 x 16 long
C	Bottom-End Cleats	2	1 x 6 x 16 long
D	Top-Front and Back Aprons	2	1 x 8 x 45 long
E	Bottom-Rear Cleat	1	1 x 6 x 45 long
F	Bottom-Front Cleat	1	1 x 6 x 43½ long
G	Top	2	2 x 10 x 60 long

40 No. 10 flathead wood screws, 1½ inches long

6 2 x 2 inch angle irons with 1-inch screws

Assemble the two end sections first. Then screw on the cleats D, E, and F. Fasten the top from below, using the angle irons. Round off all corners and edges.

YOUR TOOL BOARD

It is best to have a tool panel about 4 x 6 feet of ¾-inch plywood for tool storage. Arrange the tools as you desire, using ¼-inch dowels and 2-inch screw hooks to hold the tools. Pegboard, or perforated board, with pre-formed hooks is often suggested for a tool panel. Although the arrangement looks attractive, it is quite expensive and not practical, since a great amount of room is wasted on the board because the holes are pre-located. Also, it may be impossible to have the hook just where you want it to hold the tool in the correct position. Dowels and screw hooks allow you greater flexibility and closer grouping. Make your own rack for the chisels and other small tools as shown. See if you can locate some used nests of drawers or kitchen cabinets at remodelers or builders. They make excellent storage places for tools and other shop items.

Author's hand-tool rack, with "a place for everything and everything in its place."

Wise Tool Selection   There is a fairly wide range in tool prices and, as with other items, price usually reflects the quality of the tool. It is our suggestion, based on many years of experience, that you buy the best tool rather than the cheapest one, whenever possible, since you will get relatively more for your money. Tools last a long, long time, and the small extra cost of the better tool at the start, when spread over the years you will enjoy working with them, will come to just a few pennies a year. Again, good tools, pleasant working conditions, and initial success may lead you into wider woodworking operations, such as building cabinets, furniture, even boats—who can tell? If this happens, you will always thank yourself for getting good tools at the start. Think it over!

HAND TOOLS NEEDED

Listed below are the basic hand-woodworking tools that will allow you to handle all the operations necessary for making toys. They also are the basic tools for all woodworking. Nine chances out of ten you already have some of these, so it will not be necessary to buy all of them at once. As you expand your projects you may want to get additional items. Only your experience will tell you what you want and need.

Get a catalog from a better mail-order house, visit your local hardware or department store, and you will find what you want.

An Important Suggestion: No matter what the quality of the tools you have, *keep them razor sharp at all times.* There are several reasons for this. A sharp tool does a better, more accurate job. And a sharp tool is a *safe* tool. Dull tools are dangerous.

THE BASIC TOOL LIST

26-inch hand crosscut saw	Pencil compass and scriber
14-inch backsaw	10-inch wood rasps, flat and round
6½-inch coping saw with blades	Pliers
7-inch block plane	⅛-inch nail set
Combination square	Marking gauge
Rule	Pocket knife
Hand brace	C clamps, 2- and 4-inch, two of each
Auger bits, ¼-, ⅜-, ½-, ¾-, and 1-inch sizes	Combination sharpening stone
Hand drill	Sandpaper, medium and fine
Drill bits, 1/16- through 11/16-inch sizes	7-inch woodworker's vise for bench
Screw drivers, 3 sizes	Shop brush and dustpan
	Oilcan

When you buy your tools, try and get the best "tool clerk" or the owner of the store to wait on you. He will be of tremendous help in making the wise and correct selection of each tool.

NAILS AND SCREWS

You do not need a lot of big nails and screws when making toys; you'll find a large assortment of many sizes to be handier. However, you should have these on hand to start. As time advances, you will assemble a greater assortment.

Brads (these have small heads and are set into the wood, using the nail set). Sizes: ½, ⅝, ¾, 1, and 1¼ inches.

Nails (these have flat heads, are not set, and perhaps hold better than brads). Buy them in boxes and store them this way. Sizes: same as brads listed above.

A Suggestion: If there are public auctions of household goods in your locality, be sure to attend them. Not only will you frequently find excellent buys in hand tools, but in power tools as well. Also, you may find jars and boxes of all sorts of nails, screws, hooks, and "junk"—all very valuable to the toymaker. Sort out these finds, put small nails or brads in one jar, bigger ones into another. Flathead screws and roundheaded screws should also be stored in their own jars. It's fun sorting out these items, a good job for one or all of the kids, and it will save time when you start to build. Do the same with nuts and bolts and washers and all the other items you have and find. As a rule, do not buy boxes of screws; they cost too much this way, since you must buy such a large quantity. It is better to buy them in small lots in plastic envelopes, as displayed at the hardware store, when they are needed for the job at hand. Those not used can be added to your general screw storage jar.

To store your jars of screws and other items, make a shelf rack as shown in the photo. For a neater appearance you can add jars of similar size and shape as they are emptied in the kitchen. Baby food jars are excellent for small items.

Glass jars provide excellent storage for nails, screws, and other small items.

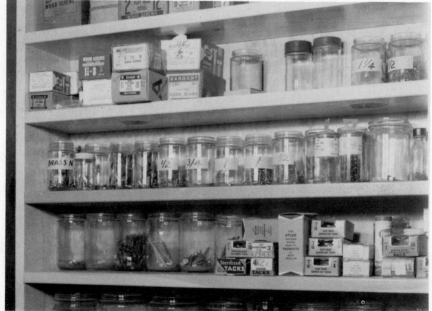

WHICH GLUE SHOULD I USE?

The answer to this often-asked question is quite simple: Use any of the popular white glues such as Elmer's Glue, U.S. Plywood Weldwood, Sear's All-Purpose White Glue, M-D Glue, or any of the hide glues. All are excellent; just follow the directions given by the manufacturer. Glueing tiny parts is not too exacting and does not require a great amount of expertise. All of these glues when used as directed will provide a bond stronger than the wood itself. Make sure that the surfaces of the wood to be glued fit perfectly, that the wood is sanded fairly smooth, and free of all wax, oil, or grease, since these glues are water soluble and will not adhere unless the surfaces are clean. Use just enough glue to cover the surfaces to be bonded. Use only a thin coat, but be sure it is spread to the very edges of the surfaces. Allow the glue to set for a short period and then press the parts together. Hold in position with a clamp—you need not use much pressure. Any glue that has escaped at the glue joint can be removed with a damp or wet cloth. Allow to dry as long a time as directed on the container.

Another popular glue is epoxy cement. As the name implies it is really a cement and can be used to bond wood, metals, fiberglass, pottery, and most plastics. It is supplied in two tubes, one resin and the other, the hardener. Appropriate amounts of each are mixed just before using. It is waterproof, but a bit expensive and not actually needed for toy-building. However, it is a nice cement to have on hand for many small minor repairs around the house. Your lumberyard, hardware or department store, or hobby shop carry all these glues and the salespeople there will be happy to help you select the one you need for your work.

A WORD ABOUT POWER TOOLS

As your interest in woodworking expands you will want to make more toys, especially if you want to make enough to sell at a profit. You will then need the assistance of power tools. You will find, too, that with the addition of these units you will be able to do much more general woodworking, such as building cabinets, small pieces of furniture, novelties of wood, and hundreds of other useful, salable items. You may also be able to cut the costs of repairs around the house, so that these tools will pay for themselves in a short time.

For simple toy-making, however, there is one power tool that will do multiple jobs. It is the scroll saw. With it you can do all sawing—straight-line as well as curved—and "inside" cutting, such as cutting the inside of an **O**. You can also file and sand with it.

For general woodworking the circular saw, or bench saw, should be the first power tool to acquire. On it you rip, crosscut, dado, miter cut, make moldings, etc. This first tool should be followed by the jointer plane, which planes surfaces and edges smooth and straight; and next, a bench grinder for keeping all tools sharp. It may be that you will want to get the bench grinder before any other power tools, since its use is so important. Then add a belt-disc sander, drill press, band saw, wood-turning lathe, and a thickness planer. A dust collector is a nice investment because it helps keeps the shop neat and clean.

A Suggestion: When working with power tools be sure to protect your face and eyes by wearing a face shield or at least a pair of shop goggles.

One of the handiest portable power tools is the electric hand drill, or "hole shooter." When mounted on a stand, it does most of the work of a drill press. A portable belt, or orbital, sander also allows you to do more work and eliminates the tedium of hand-sanding. However, they are not needed for toy-building; rather, they are used more for general woodworking.

With most power tools you have a wide assortment of accessories which greatly expand the original use of the tool; consequently, production operations can be done in your shop. Again, the tool catalogs list these helpful items. Contact your hardware store or hardware department. You will find someone there who will be of assistance to you in the proper selection.

FINISHING

This can be as simple or as complicated as you desire. **Be careful**, however, to use only those products, clear or pigmented, that are recommended by the manufacturer for use on toys, and also be sure the labels on the cans carry this guarantee. If they do not, under no circumstances should you use the product!

Hardly any pigments or other ordinary finishing products can be ingested; and since a small child has the tendency to put a toy to its mouth, there is the danger of poisoning. Better to have the toy without any finish whatsoever than to take this risk. Check and double-check. Before you purchase the product, read the label carefully, and then get the assurance and advice from your hardware, hobby, or paint dealer that the finish can be safely used on toys.

Almost every manufactured toy you see in the stores is finished with bright, gaudy colors. This is done to attract the child and is a definite plus in helping sell more toys. However, there is much more elegance, warmth, and beauty in having a wooden toy without any color. The grain of the wood is so exotic, so delicate, so beautiful, that it needs nothing more to enhance it. If you have chosen a piece of wood with a particularly nice grain, all you have to do is give it several coats of wax, and the job is completed. Or you can give it one or two coats of spray or brushing lacquer.

For best results, sand the finished parts to perfection. Use the medium-grit sandpaper first; finish off with fine grit. If possible, sand the parts before assembling them into the finished toy. By doing this, you can get into every corner and surface, and the finished toy will look so much better. In using lacquer, you do not have to finish the entire part because the lacquer dries so quickly. Finish or coat as much as you can at one time, leaving one edge or surface "raw," and place the part on this raw side to dry. When the rest of the toy is dry, this side can then be lacquered. This same procedure may be followed if varnish or paint is used. There are any number of quick-drying, clear, transparent finishes on the market, which your dealer can tell you about.

Wax Finish   One of the simplest finishes for toys is regular furniture polish wax. This can be ordinary paste wax, available in cans or in aerosol spray cans. Before the wax is applied, the toy parts or the completed toy should be sanded perfectly smooth, using fine sandpaper or extra-fine steel wool. Then apply several coats of wax. Toys with a wax finish are easy to keep clean and simple to refinish by just washing them and then giving them another coat of wax. The more wax coats you give them, the more durable the finish. Be sure the wax is safe for toys.

When a finish is applied, it may raise the grain of the wood. To overcome this, sand again, then use fine steel wool to produce a smooth surface. The roughness is often more noticeable on the end grain of the wood, so be certain these areas are as smooth as possible before the finish is applied.

HANDMADE WOODEN TOYS—A SOURCE OF ADDITIONAL INCOME

As mentioned before, making your own toys is a nice, pleasant way to save money, and the toy designs in this book are for your personal use. However, you could very well make toys for selling at a handsome profit. This can be done in several ways: You could sell them to friends and relatives, for they too would like to save some money. Further, they would have the assurance that the toys you supplied would last and last, and not come apart or break after just a little use. Their children would not only like these toys, but be proud and appreciative of them. We know of several cases in which these toys are considered "special" by the little ones, who give them extra care and attention. We even know of one instance where a toy such as this was given its own shelf on which to stand, and thus it serves as a room display when not being played with. Until you have experienced it yourself, you have no idea of what a good feeling it is to see one of your creations given this loving care and attention!

A Serious Suggestion: Before you attempt to sell any toys be sure they meet all of the standards set forth in the Banned Toy List of the Consumer Product Safety Commission, Washington, D.C. 20207. Write to them for a free copy of this list. Also check all local and regional codes, which in some areas are quite stringent. It is better to do this before you start than to have a big stock of toys on hand that cannot be sold. Check this out thoroughly.

In making toys for sale you should keep track of your time, the cost of materials, light, etc., in order to determine the price you should charge for them. Even at a rough estimate you should make a nice profit. However, do not plan on becoming rich or making a fortune—you'll not do that. But you will do this: You will be turning otherwise idle, wasted time into real dollars. We have seen this happen over and over. Every dollar you make you can invest, if you desire, in more and better power tools or hand tools.

Another possibility to investigate is that of supplying these toys to the better shops in your locality. You will be surprised at what a demand you can create here! Pick the best shop you can, and give them a dozen toys or so on consignment at the start. Ask the merchant to display them and to give them some publicity in the local paper or to plug them over local radio. Better yet, have him get a word-of-mouth campaign started. If the shop is the best outlet, the owner or manager will know what and how to do it. He or she will be only too anxious to have this exclusive outlet for your toys and will have no problem selling them.

If you intend to get into the business of toy-making in a serious way, it would be wise to have your attorney help you arrange all the details of this setup properly.

How to Make Wheels   Wheels are an integral part of most toys, and in Part 2 of this book we show you all the practical ways to make them. This is the only book we know of in which this important subject is completely covered, from hand-cut wheels to machine-cut ones. You will receive great assistance here.

Enjoy a Double Reward   As you progress with your toy-making, you will begin to think of your tools, both hand and power, as *your* "toys." They will bring you relaxation, enjoyment, and a new outlook on life. The other reward is that the products of your handiwork, the toys you give your children, will bring them happiness too. And you can't do better than that, now, can you?

Part 1
TOYS AND DESIGNS

How to Enlarge or Reduce a Design or Drawing

To enlarge a design, mark it into squares as shown, or mark the squares on a piece of tracing paper or acetate. If the design is to be twice as large as the original, draw squares twice as large. Where the lines of the design cross the lines of the square, mark an **X** on the larger squares. Then connect these points with a light, fine line and complete the pattern with a heavy line as shown below. To reduce a design, draw the squares smaller than those of the original design.

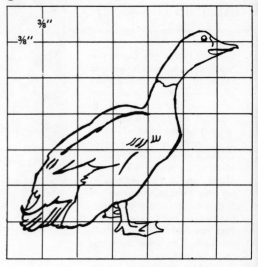

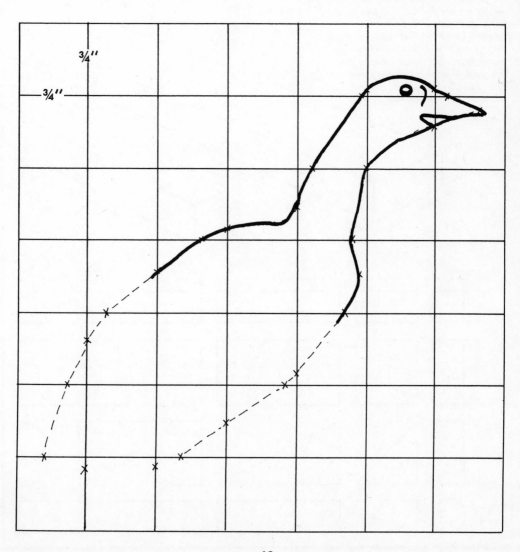

BUILDING BLOCKS

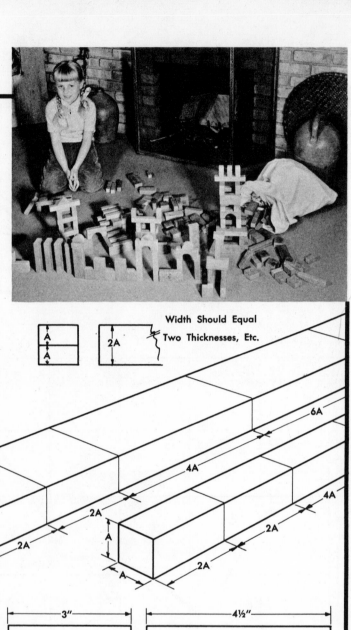

Building blocks are a popular toy that youngsters put to thousands of uses. The sizes of the individual pieces must be based on a common dimension, usually the thickness of the lumber used. Thus, if ¾-in. lumber is used, the other dimensions must be multiples of ¾ in., such as 1½ in., 3 in., 4½ in., etc. Before starting to cut the lumber, measure its thickness accurately and then cut one or two pieces to see that you have the correct dimensions. The lower drawings show dimensions based on ¾-in. lumber. The blocks can be easily cut on the circular saw with the use of a hollow ground blade or they can be cut by hand with the aid of a miter box. Soft pine should be used. The round blocks are cut from ¾-in. dowel. Make at least 25 of each size.

Width Should Equal
Two Thicknesses, Etc.

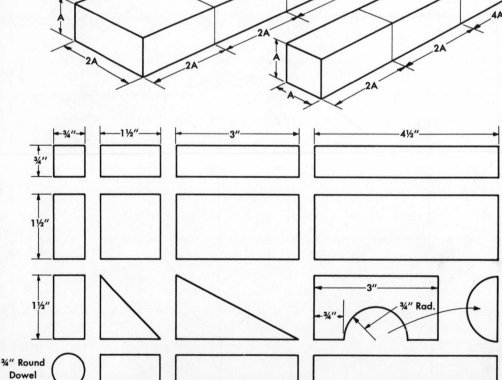

¾" Round Dowel

TRIANGLE DESIGN BLOCKS

These easily made blocks will provide countless hours of fun for boys and girls. Shown are just a few of the many beautiful and interesting designs that can be made. Use ¾-in. stock; white pine is best but any other wood can be used. The size shown is convenient for a small child to play with, but the blocks can be made larger or smaller as desired. In painting them, use several brilliant colors such as red, blue, green, and yellow. An excellent Christmas gift.

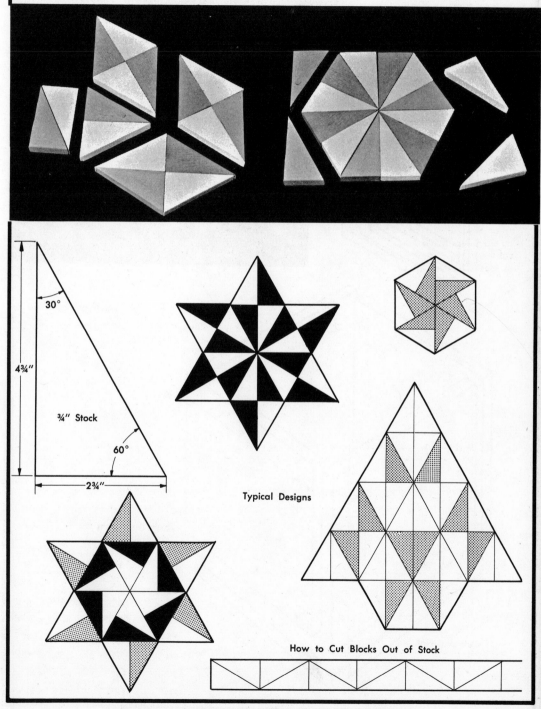

30°

4¾"

¾" Stock

60°

2¾"

Typical Designs

How to Cut Blocks Out of Stock

Boxes always intrigue small children because so many things can be built with them. They become a stairway, a barn, a house; they can be piled on top of one another to make a mountain. These boxes will be sturdy if they are made of ½-in. plywood, securely glued and nailed together. The pieces should be cut accurately. The table below gives the dimensions for a nest of eight different sizes that fit together for simple storage. The boxes can be enameled in bright colors.

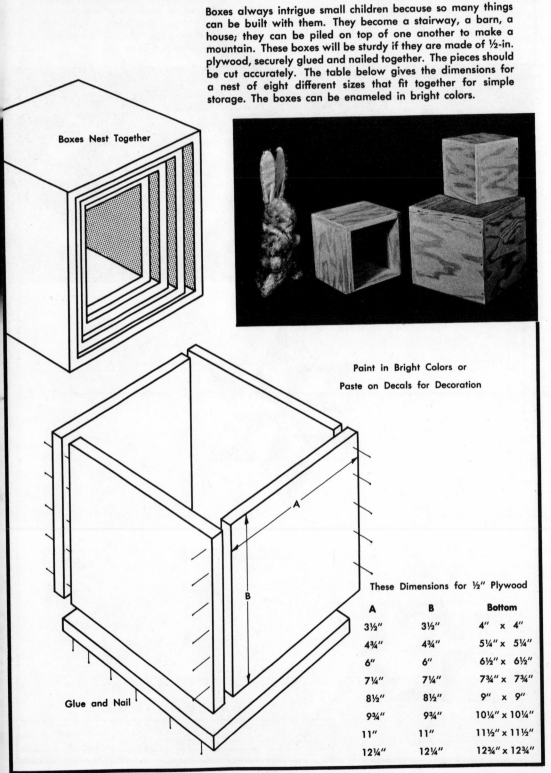

Boxes Nest Together

Paint in Bright Colors or

Paste on Decals for Decoration

A

B

Glue and Nail

These Dimensions for ½" Plywood

A	B	Bottom
3½"	3½"	4" x 4"
4¾"	4¾"	5¼" x 5¼"
6"	6"	6½" x 6½"
7¼"	7¼"	7¾" x 7¾"
8½"	8½"	9" x 9"
9¾"	9¾"	10¼" x 10¼"
11"	11"	11½" x 11½"
12¼"	12¼"	12¾" x 12¾"

STICK-TOGETHER BLOCKS

These blocks are easy to make, yet they stimulate a child's imagination and provide an endless variety of shapes and designs. Anything from grotesque animals to space ships can be put together in minutes. Use any scrap lumber available. Close-grain woods such as pine, basswood, or maple are best. Typical shapes and sizes are shown. Devise your own if you desire. Make at least ½ dozen of each, the more the better. All holes are ¼ in. Make ten ¼-in. hardwood dowels. The blocks can be dyed in bright colors. If painted, do not get paint in the holes and do not use on the dowels.

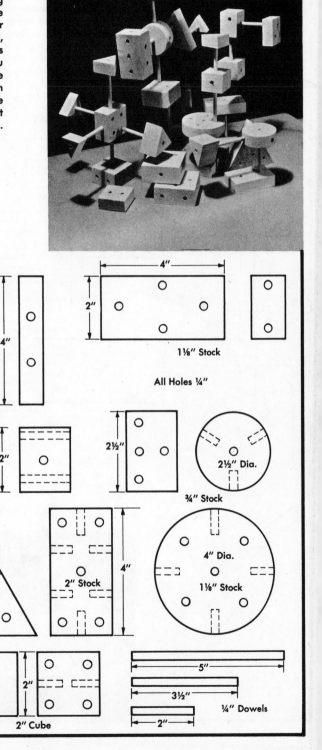

6"

4"

¾" Stock

4"

4"

2"

1⅛" Stock

All Holes ¼"

2"

2"

2"

2"

2"

2½"

2½" Dia.

¾" Stock

2½"

2½"

4"

4"

2" Stock

4" Dia.

1⅛" Stock

4"

1½"

2"

2" Cube

5"

3½"

¼" Dowels

2"

17

PUT-TOGETHER BLOCKS

These easily made blocks will provide children with many hours of pleasure. They can be put together in countless combinations. The set consists of grooved blocks and flat boards best made of wallboard or composition board. Scraps can be used to good advantage, but the boards must be of the same thickness so that they fit snugly into the grooves. The blocks can be made of pine. The grooves are cut on the circular saw with the use of the dado head. Shapes other than those shown also can be used. Make at least six of each type and size of block and board.

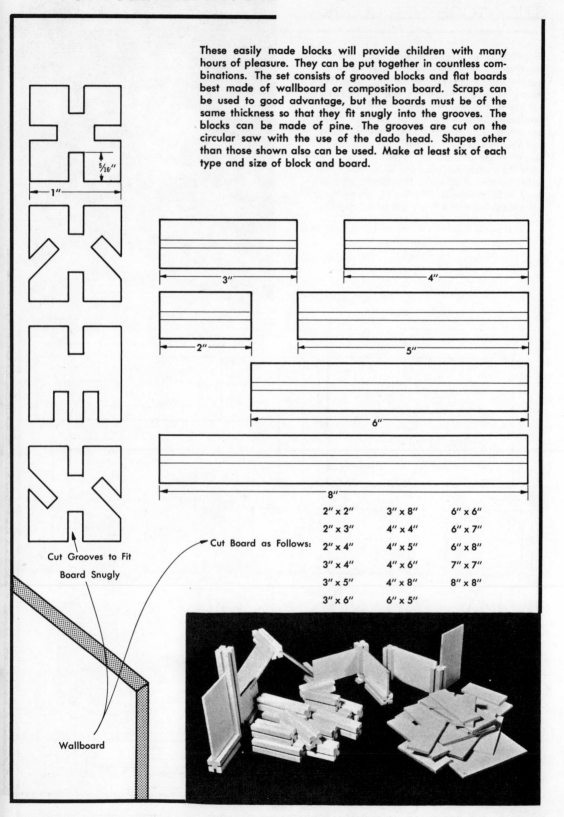

5/16"

1"

3"

4"

2"

5"

6"

8"

Cut Board as Follows:

2" x 2"	3" x 8"	6" x 6"
2" x 3"	4" x 4"	6" x 7"
2" x 4"	4" x 5"	6" x 8"
3" x 4"	4" x 6"	7" x 7"
3" x 5"	4" x 8"	8" x 8"
3" x 6"	6" x 5"	

Cut Grooves to Fit
Board Snugly

Wallboard

MAGIC CUBES

Youngsters from six to sixty like to play with these colored cubes. They are a good test of one's imagination. Many interesting combinations can be made. Arrange a design in the box, close it, and turn it over to see what the reverse side is like! Surprising! Be very careful in making the cubes. If the dimensions of all the sides are not exact, the cubes will not fit correctly in the box. For best results, use hardwood such as maple. Make the cubes first and then construct the box to fit, making the sides and ends high enough to allow for the saw kerf. Put the box together; then saw through it, dividing it into two parts. Be sure to paint the cubes as indicated. Draw your favorite designs on paper and paste it on the inside of the cover and bottom of the box as illustrated.

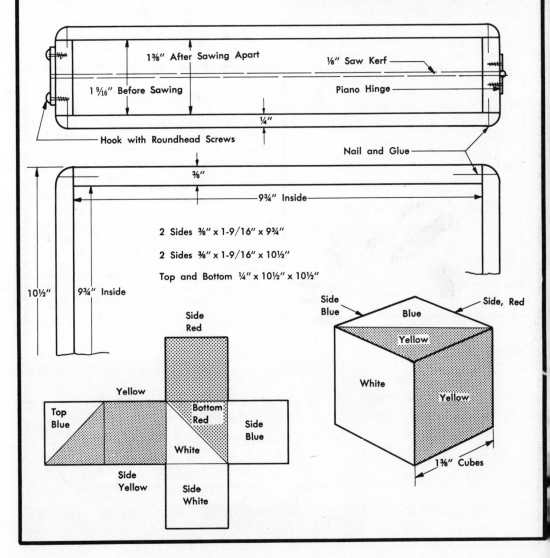

1⅜" After Sawing Apart

⅛" Saw Kerf

1 9/16" Before Sawing

Piano Hinge

¼"

Hook with Roundhead Screws

Nail and Glue

⅜"

9¾" Inside

2 Sides ⅜" x 1-9/16" x 9¾"

2 Sides ⅜" x 1-9/16" x 10½"

Top and Bottom ¼" x 10½" x 10½"

10½"

9¾" Inside

Side Red

Yellow

Top Blue

Bottom Red

Side Blue

White

Side Yellow

Side White

Side Blue

Side, Red

Blue

Yellow

White

Yellow

1⅜" Cubes

THE FLEET'S IN!

With a handful of scrap lumber, and in just one evening, a whole fleet can be built as shown above. Establish a center line on the piece of stock and then, using an irregular curve, scribe the shape of the ship. If you have a band saw or scroll saw, tilt the table a few degrees when cutting the angle — this adds realism to the finished ships. Use other scrap stock for the cabins and super-structures and 5/16-in. dowels for the stacks. Paint or enamel the completed boats in gay, bright colors.

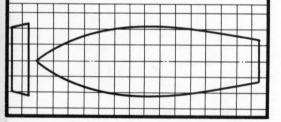

CARS GALORE

A Cadillac, a Lincoln, an Imperial — Buicks, Fords, Chevys — almost any make and model the youngster wants may be had. This is a very old idea but it has not been used to any great extent lately. The cars you see here are taken from current, four-color advertisements of automobiles appearing in magazines. The pictures are pasted on heavy cardboard, composition board, or light plywood with the use of rubber cement. They are then cut out with a coping saw or scroll saw. To make them stand upright, glue one or two blocks on the reverse side. True, they are "one-sided" but few "young drivers" care about this. Some of the models are 20 in. long.

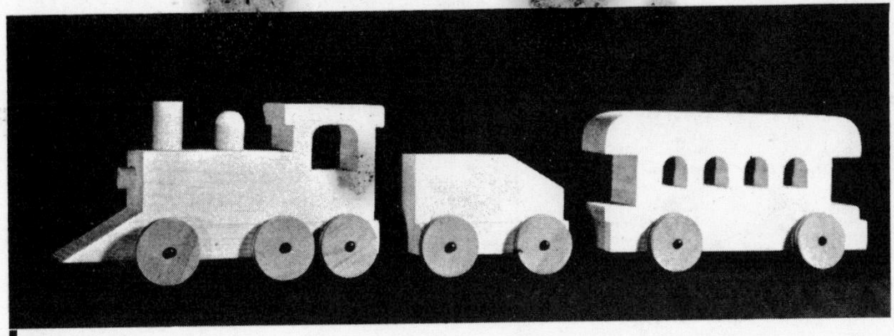

2 x 4 TRAIN

This train is so called because it is made of a standard 2 x 4 which, as you know, measures approximately 1⅝ by 3⅝ in. Since your stock may not be exactly this size, the dimensions may be varied accordingly. The windows are made by boring ¾-in. holes and then jigsawing out the rest of the stock. A ⅜ x ¾-in. strip is nailed along the bottom side edge of each unit. The wheels are made of ⅜-in. plywood, 1½ in. in diameter. Drill the holes so that the wheels turn freely. The cars are coupled by means of ordinary screw eyes and screw hooks as shown. The smokestack, sand dome, and headlight are made of dowels. Paint the entire assembly in bright, attractive colors and put a pull string on the locomotive.

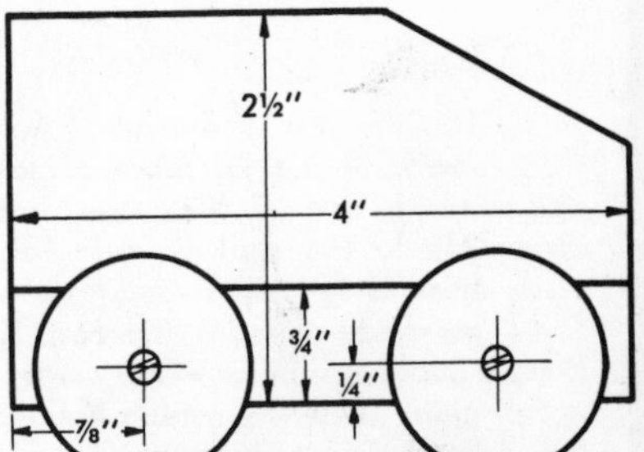

2½″
4″
¾″
¼″
⅞″

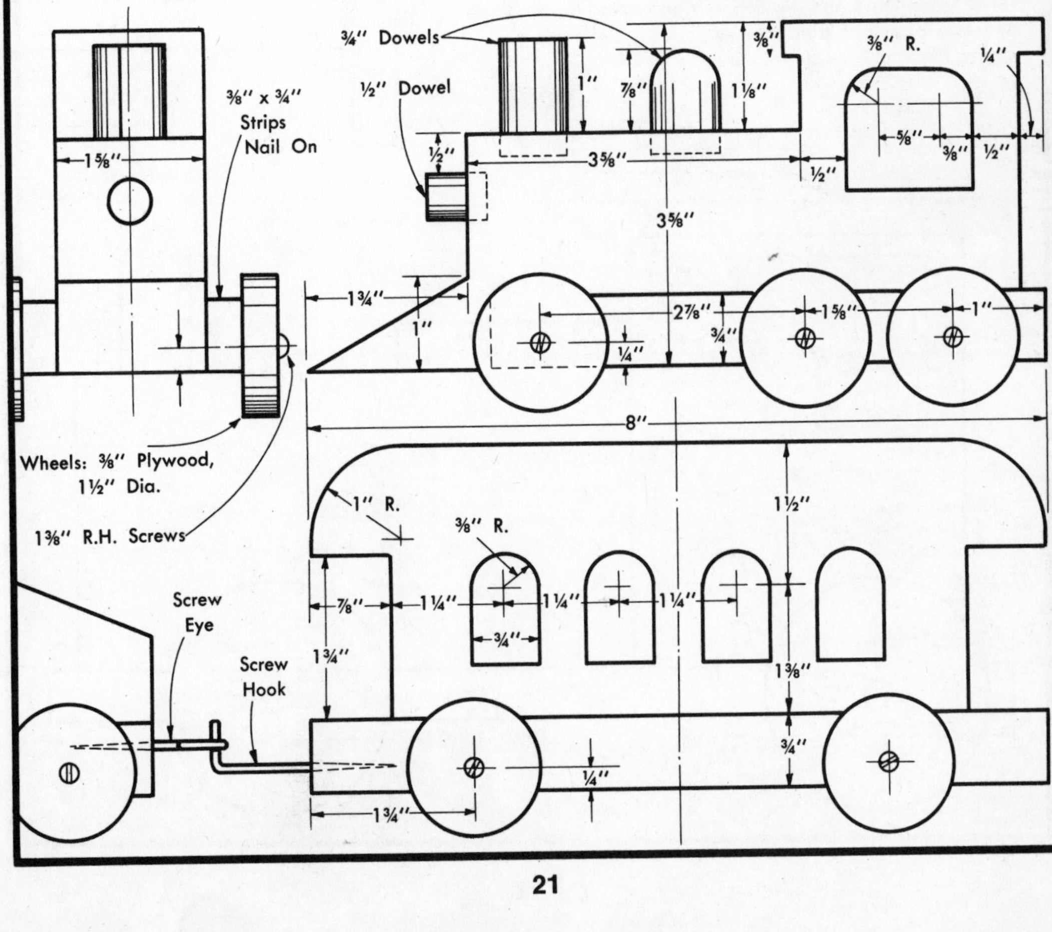

¾″ Dowels
½″ Dowel
⅜″ x ¾″ Strips Nail On
1⅝″
1″
⅞″
1⅛″
⅜″
⅜″ R.
¼″
½″
3⅝″
⅝″
⅜″
½″
½″
3⅝″
1¾″
1″
2⅞″
1⅝″
1″
¾″
¼″
8″
Wheels: ⅜″ Plywood, 1½″ Dia.
1⅜″ R.H. Screws
1″ R.
⅜″ R.
1½″
⅞″
1¼″
1¼″
1¼″
¾″
Screw Eye
Screw Hook
1¾″
1⅜″
¾″
¼″
1¾″

HUSKY LOCOMOTIVE

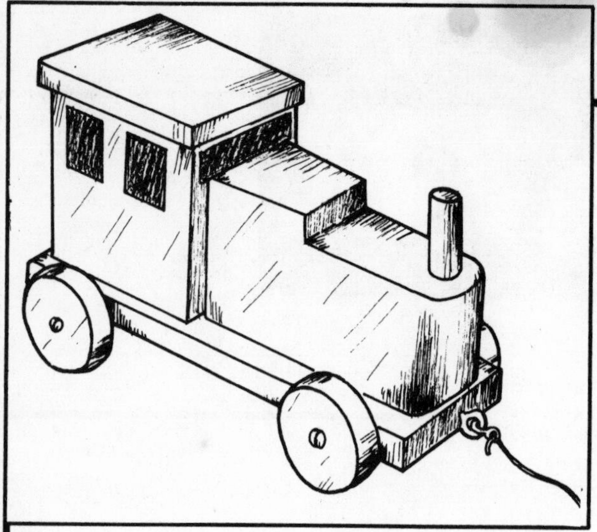

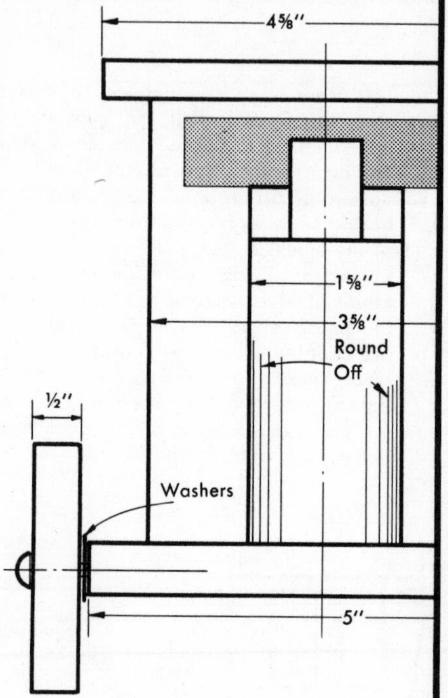
4⅝"
1⅝"
3⅝"
Round Off
½"
Washers
5"

This toy will take a lot of hard use since it is made of a solid piece of scrap 4 x 4 (3⅝ x 3⅝") and a 6-in. piece of 2 x 4 (1⅝" x 3⅝"). The roof is ⅜-in. plywood and the base is ½-in. plywood. The wheels may also be made of ½-in. plywood. The locomotive is simple to build. The parts are nailed together with the wheels held by 1¾-in. roundhead screws. Paint the assembled toy in bright colors and add a screw eye and string to make it a prized pull toy.

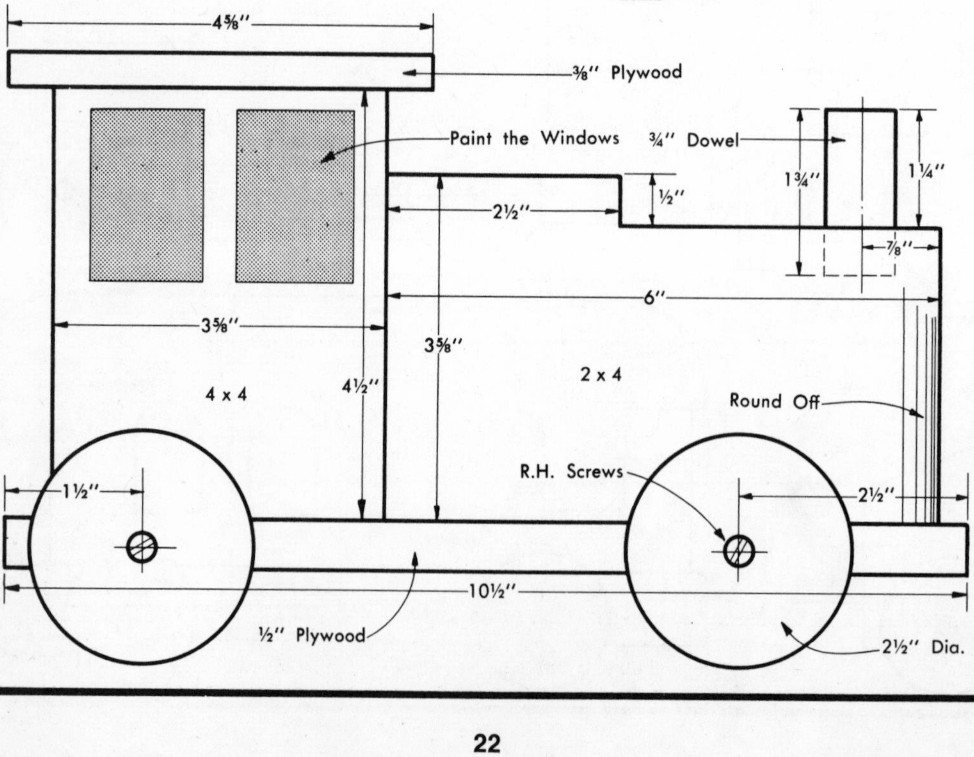
4⅝"
⅜" Plywood
Paint the Windows
¾" Dowel
1¾"
1¼"
½"
2½"
⅞"
6"
3⅝"
3⅝"
4½"
4 x 4
2 x 4
Round Off
R.H. Screws
1½"
2½"
10½"
½" Plywood
2½" Dia.

DUMP TRUCK

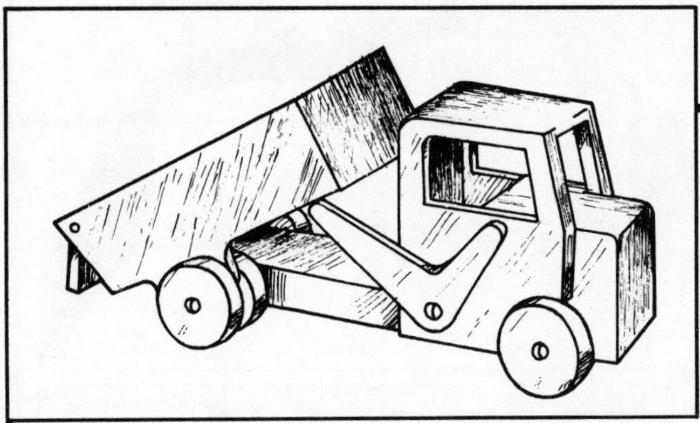

The dual rear wheels and tires and the dump lever which tilts the dump body give this sturdy toy a touch of realism that any boy will appreciate. The truck is quite simple to build. The cab and body are made of ¼-in. plywood. The undercarriage may be made of standard 2-in. plank (1⅝ in. thick). See that the tail gate swings freely on the nail pivots and that the dump body rotates freely on the axle screws.

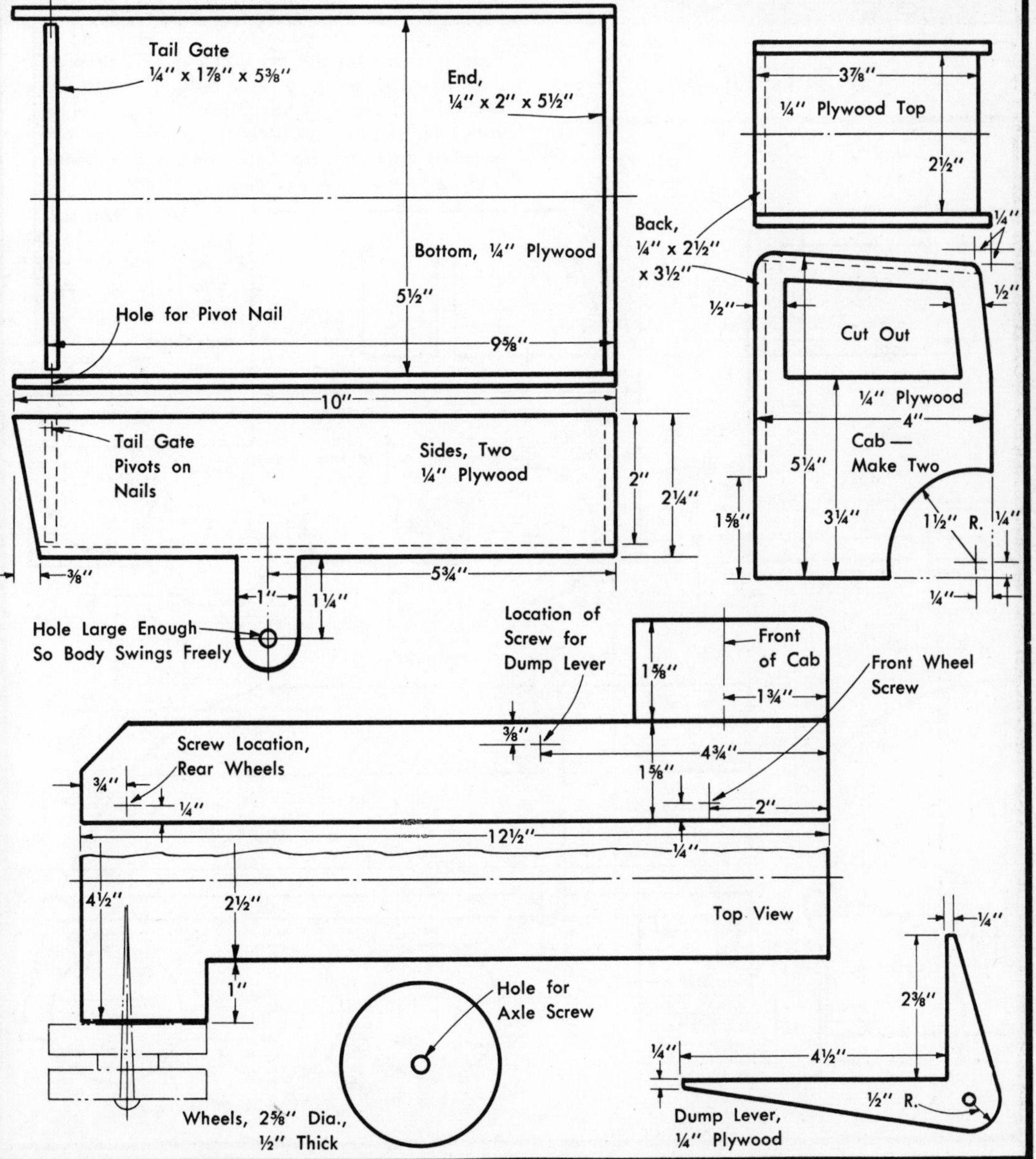
Tail Gate
¼" x 1⅞" x 5⅜"
End,
¼" x 2" x 5½"
Bottom, ¼" Plywood
5½"
Hole for Pivot Nail
9⅝"
10"
Tail Gate Pivots on Nails
Sides, Two
¼" Plywood
2"
2¼"
⅜"
5¾"
1"
1¼"
Hole Large Enough So Body Swings Freely
3⅞"
¼" Plywood Top
2½"
¼"
Back,
¼" x 2½"
x 3½"
½"
½"
Cut Out
¼" Plywood
4"
Cab —
Make Two
5¼"
3¼"
1⅝"
1½" R.
¼"
¼"
Location of Screw for Dump Lever
Front of Cab
1⅝"
1¾"
Front Wheel Screw
⅜"
4¾"
Screw Location, Rear Wheels
¾"
¼"
1⅝"
2"
12½"
¼"
4½"
2½"
Top View
1"
Hole for Axle Screw
Wheels, 2⅝" Dia.,
½" Thick
¼"
2⅜"
¼"
4½"
½" R.
Dump Lever,
¼" Plywood

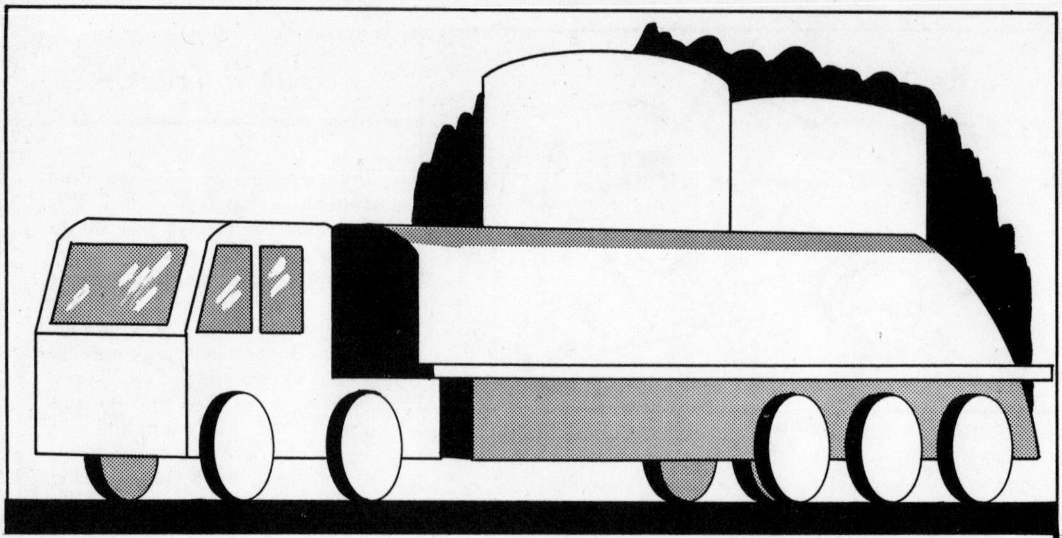

GAS TRUCK

Here is a simple project that can be made in one evening to give hundreds of hours of pleasure. Use soft pine. Paint in bright colors with windows in dark blue. If available, cut out gasoline company trademarks from magazines and paste onto the cab and truck body.

Bill of Materials

Cab	3¾″ x 4″ x 6¾″
Truck	3¾″ x 4″ x 12″
Wheels	2″ dia. x ½″
Dowel	¼″ x 1″
Side Strips	¼″ x ¼″ x 11¾″

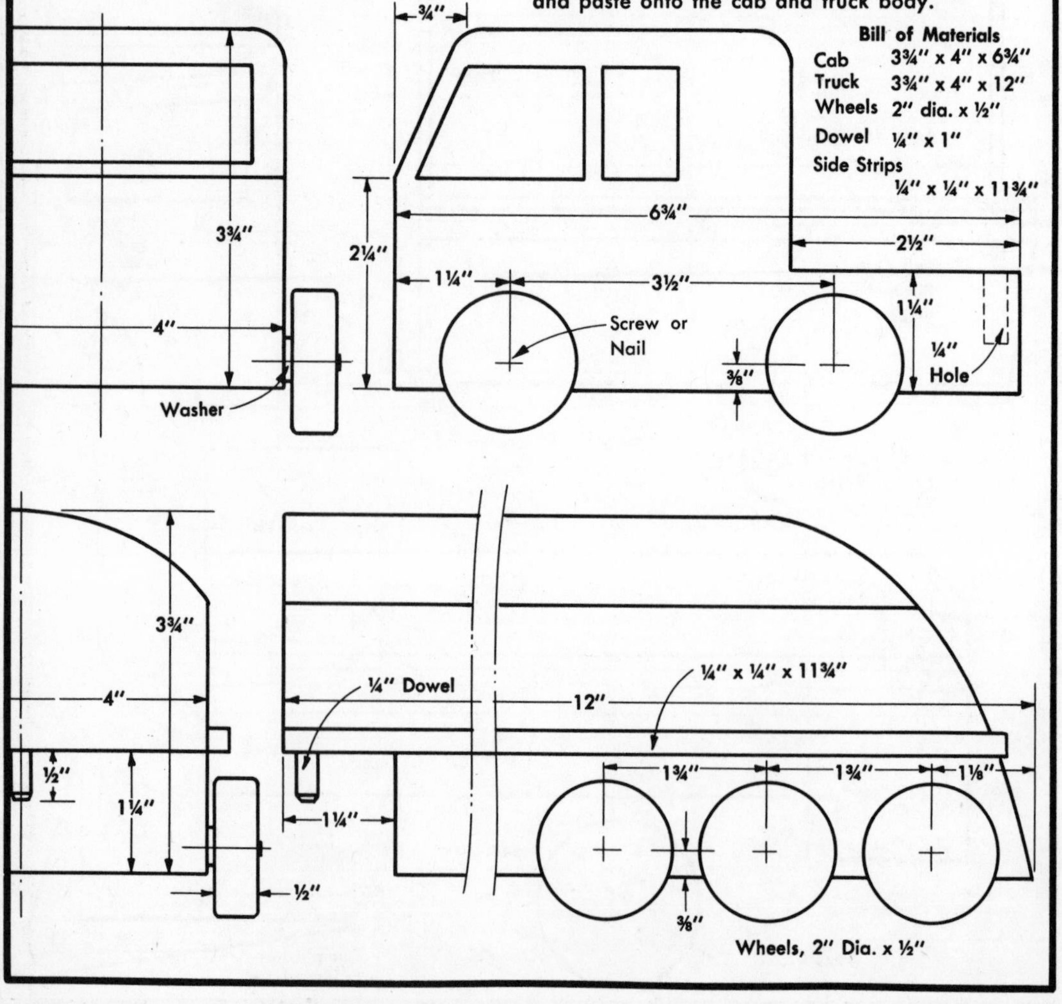

¾″
3¾″
2¼″
6¾″
2½″
1¼″
3½″
4″
Screw or Nail
1¼″
⅜″
¼″ Hole
Washer
3¾″
¼″ Dowel
¼″ x ¼″ x 11¾″
4″
12″
½″
1¼″
1¾″
1¾″
1⅛″
1¼″
½″
⅜″
Wheels, 2″ Dia. x ½″

TRAMP FREIGHTER

This nice toy may be made of scrap ¾-in. lumber or plywood. Make the bottom first and cut out the openings for the wheels. Make the axles out of coat-hanger wire, being sure to drill a hole for a snug fit in the bottom board with a slightly larger hole in the wheel so that it turns easily. Use a washer on each side of each wheel. Next make the two cut-out sections for the hull of the boat and finally make the top deck.

This is not a boat to put in the water but rather to use indoors on the floor. Pull it with a string. The boat may be painted all white with a red deck and black trim. Try various combinations of colors and see how attractive it will be.

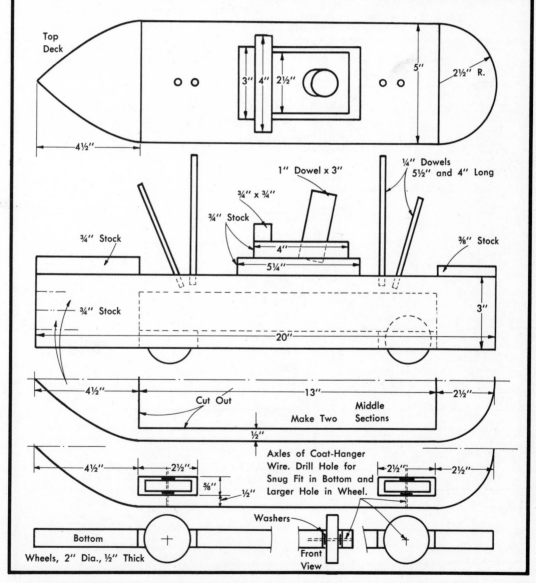

Top Deck

3" 4" 2½"

5"

2½" R.

4½"

1" Dowel x 3"

¼" Dowels
5½" and 4" Long

¾" x ¾"

¾" Stock

¾" Stock

⅜" Stock

4"

5¼"

¾" Stock

3"

20"

4½"

13"

2½"

Cut Out

Middle   Sections
Make Two

½"

Axles of Coat-Hanger
Wire. Drill Hole for
Snug Fit in Bottom and
Larger Hole in Wheel.

4½"

2½"

⅝"

½"

2½"

2½"

Washers

Bottom

Wheels, 2" Dia., ½" Thick

Front
View

TUG AND BARGE

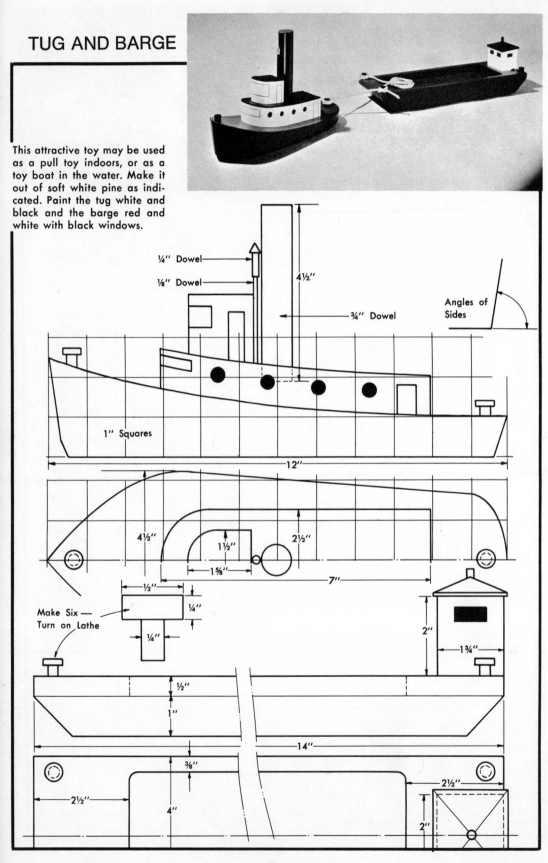

This attractive toy may be used as a pull toy indoors, or as a toy boat in the water. Make it out of soft white pine as indicated. Paint the tug white and black and the barge red and white with black windows.

¼" Dowel

⅛" Dowel

4½"

¾" Dowel

Angles of Sides

1" Squares

12"

4½"

1½"

2½"

1⅝"

7"

Make Six — Turn on Lathe

½"

¼"

¼"

2"

1¾"

½"

1"

14"

⅜"

2½"

4"

2½"

2"

TUGBOAT

Use white pine. Lay out the body of the boat on 1⅜-in. stock. First cut out the interior on a jig saw. Then nail the ½-in. board for the bottom and cut the outside form of the boat. Be sure the nails are not in the path of the blade. Taper the top of the boat from the front to the rear. Build the cabins, nail them together, paint the inside white, and nail to the deck with fine brads. Use waterproof glue if it is available. Taper the mast, drill a ¼-in. hole in the top cabin and deck, and nail it in place. Paint black with gray trim; make the cabins white.

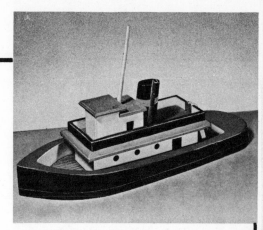

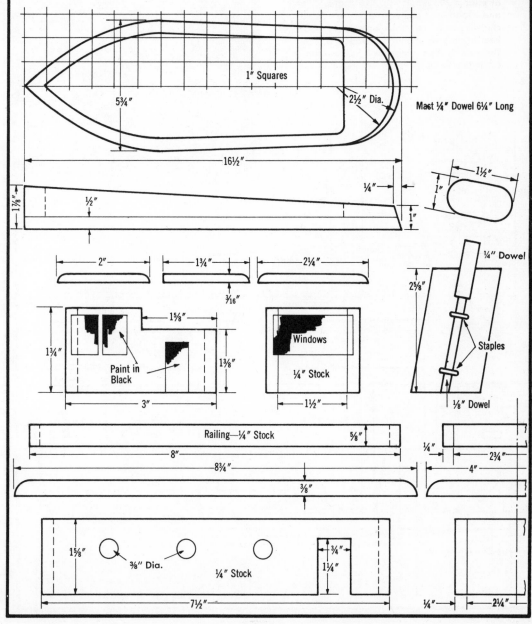

1" Squares

5¾"

2½" Dia.

Mast ¼" Dowel 6¼" Long

16½"

1⅞"

½"

¼"

1"

1½"

1"

2"

1¾"

2¼"

3/16"

¼" Dowel

1⅝"

Paint in Black

1¾"

1⅜"

Windows

¼" Stock

2⅝"

Staples

3"

1½"

⅛" Dowel

Railing—¼" Stock

⅝"

¼"

8"

2¾"

8¾"

4"

⅜"

1⅝"

⅜" Dia.

¼" Stock

¾"

1¼"

7½"

¼"

2¼"

HOBBYHORSE CART

Historians trace the hobbyhorse to pre-Christian days which perhaps makes it one of the oldest toys known. It is still popular today and affords countless hours of pleasant pastime and imaginative play. This version of the traditional hobbyhorse has a cart in which other toys may be hauled about. Construction presents no unusual problems. Use white pine for all parts except the cart which is made of plywood. The entire assembly is glued and nailed together. To add realism, include leather straps on the horse's head, held in place with brass upholstery nails. The young lady shown has added a shoe-string rein. Use heavy screws in the wheels for axles. Paint in bright colors.

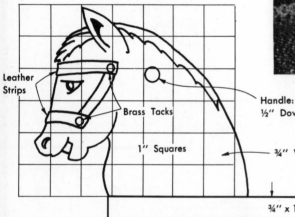

Leather Strips

Brass Tacks

1" Squares

Handle:
½" Dowel, 7" Long

¾" White Pine

¾" x 1¼" Wide

31"

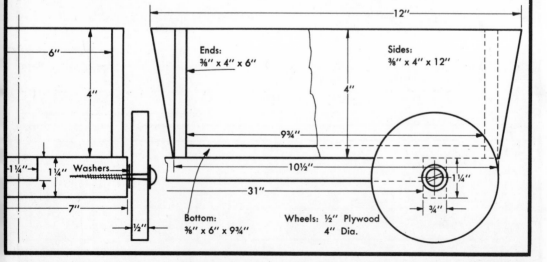

12"

6"

4"

Ends:
⅜" x 4" x 6"

Sides:
⅜" x 4" x 12"

4"

9¾"

1¼"

1¼" Washers

10½"

31"

1¼"

7"

½"

¾"

Bottom:
⅜" x 6" x 9¾"

Wheels: ½" Plywood
4" Dia.

PULL CHICKEN

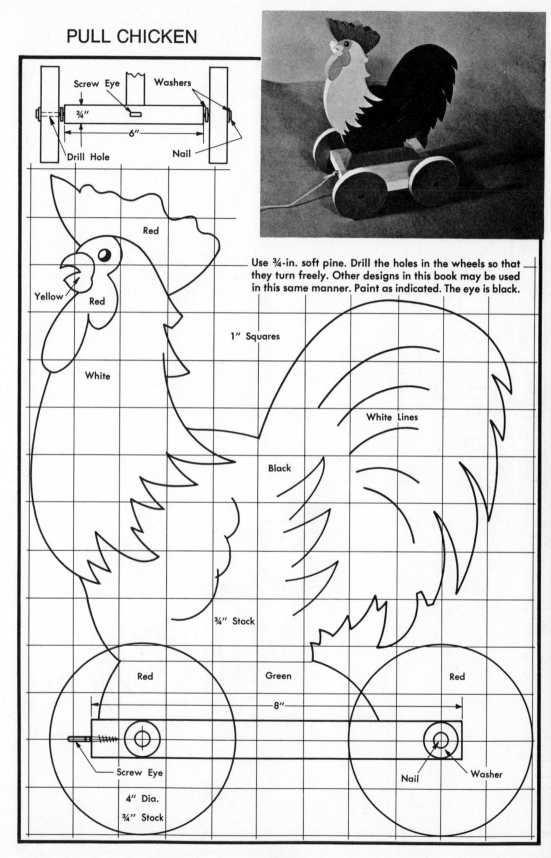

Screw Eye   Washers

¾"

6"

Drill Hole   Nail

Red

Yellow   Red

White

1" Squares

White Lines

Black

¾" Stock

Use ¾-in. soft pine. Drill the holes in the wheels so that they turn freely. Other designs in this book may be used in this same manner. Paint as indicated. The eye is black.

Red   Green   Red

8"

Screw Eye

Nail   Washer

4" Dia.

¾" Stock

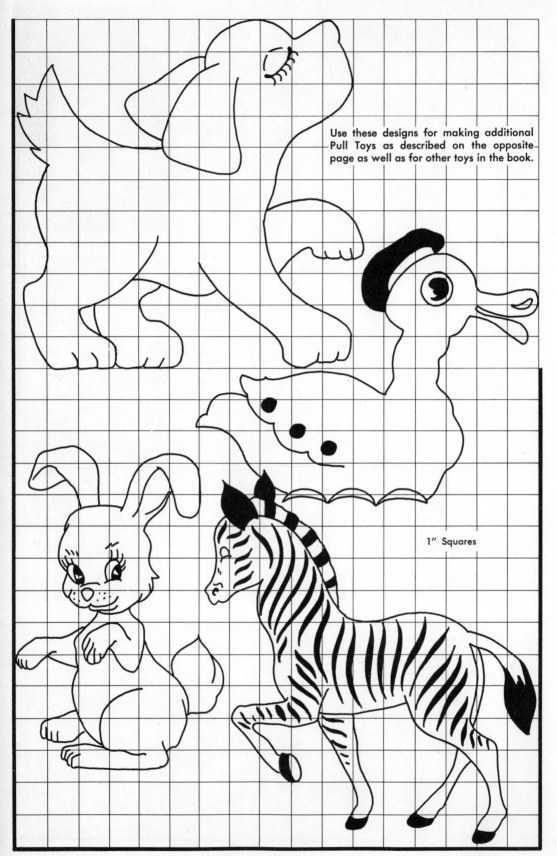

Use these designs for making additional Pull Toys as described on the opposite page as well as for other toys in the book.

1" Squares

JUMPY

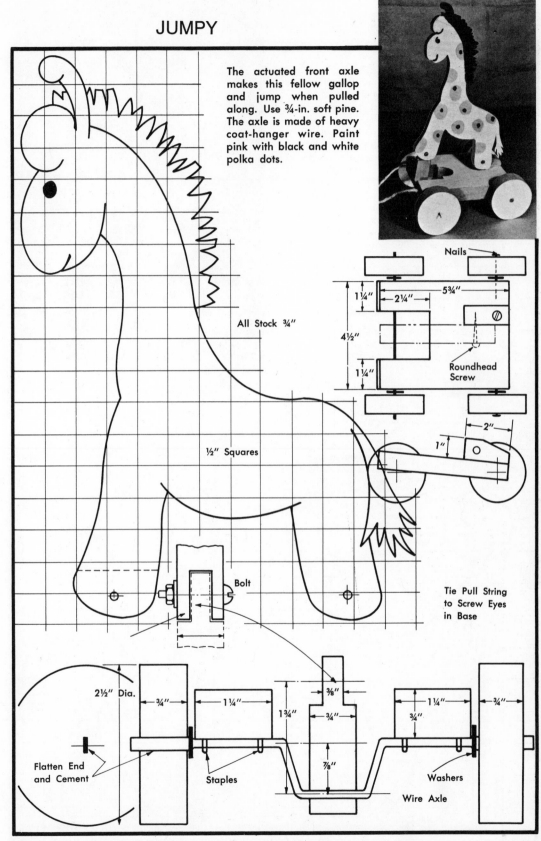

The actuated front axle makes this fellow gallop and jump when pulled along. Use ¾-in. soft pine. The axle is made of heavy coat-hanger wire. Paint pink with black and white polka dots.

All Stock ¾"

½" Squares

Nails

1¼"

2¼"

5¾"

4½"

1¼"

Roundhead Screw

2"

1"

Bolt

Tie Pull String to Screw Eyes in Base

2½" Dia.

¾"

1¼"

⅜"

1¾"

¾"

1¼"

¾"

¾"

7⁄8"

Flatten End and Cement

Staples

Wire Axle

Washers

BOB-UP DUCK

The off-center wheel in the tail of the duck makes the bird bob up and down with a nice wobble. To get this effect be sure to make the wheel 3 in. in diameter and have the axle hole exactly ½ in. off center. If it is more than this or less than this it will not turn. Dado or rout out the body of the duck figure as indicated to make room for the wheel. Make the base and figure out of ¾-in. stock. The wheels are ½-in. stock. Paint the figure white with a yellow bill. For variety, you can replace the duck figure with any other figure you find in this book.

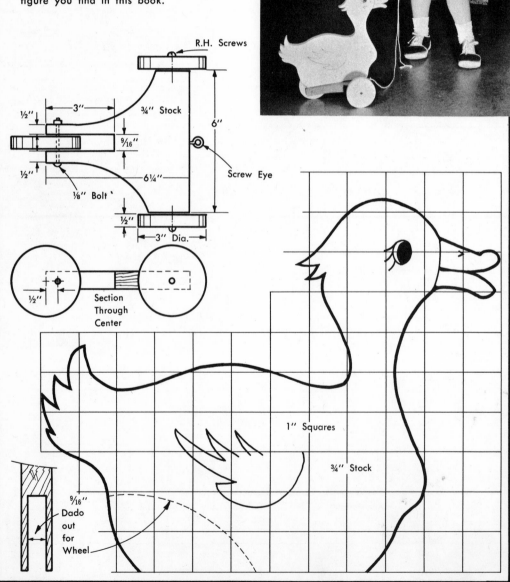

R.H. Screws

¾" Stock

3"

½"

9/16"

½"

⅛" Bolt

6"

6¼"

Screw Eye

½"

3" Dia.

½"

Section Through Center

1" Squares

¾" Stock

9/16"
Dado out for Wheel

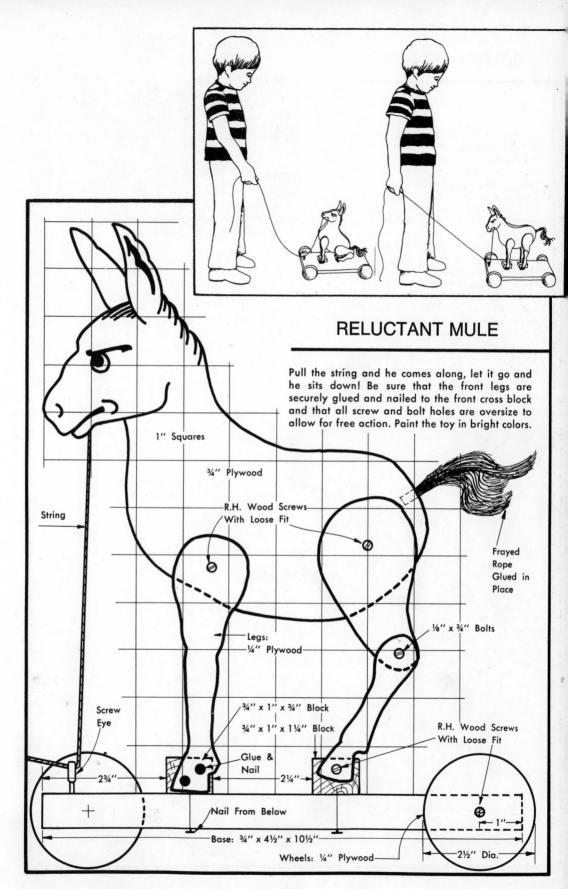

RELUCTANT MULE

Pull the string and he comes along, let it go and he sits down! Be sure that the front legs are securely glued and nailed to the front cross block and that all screw and bolt holes are oversize to allow for free action. Paint the toy in bright colors.

1" Squares

¾" Plywood

R.H. Wood Screws With Loose Fit

String

Legs: ¼" Plywood

Frayed Rope Glued in Place

⅛" x ¾" Bolts

Screw Eye

¾" x 1" x ¾" Block

¾" x 1" x 1¼" Block

Glue & Nail

R.H. Wood Screws With Loose Fit

2¾"

2¼"

1"

Nail From Below

Base: ¾" x 4½" x 10½"

Wheels: ¼" Plywood

2½" Dia.

HOOTENANNY

As this toy is pushed along the floor, the wheels with the roller at the eccentric location actuate the neck and head so that the head pops in and out. The toy is quite simple to make but special care must be taken to make the roller accurately. The ¼-in. dowel shaft is held tightly in the wheels, but the ¾-in. dowel roller must have a very loose fit over the shaft so that it rotates freely. In turn, the roller is fastened tightly to the neckpiece. All stock is ⅜-in. plywood with the exception of the head, which is ¾-in. thick. The handle is ¼-in. dowel 24 in. long. The wheels are held to the sides by means of ⅛-in. bolts using double washers. The toy may be painted with any gay colors desired.

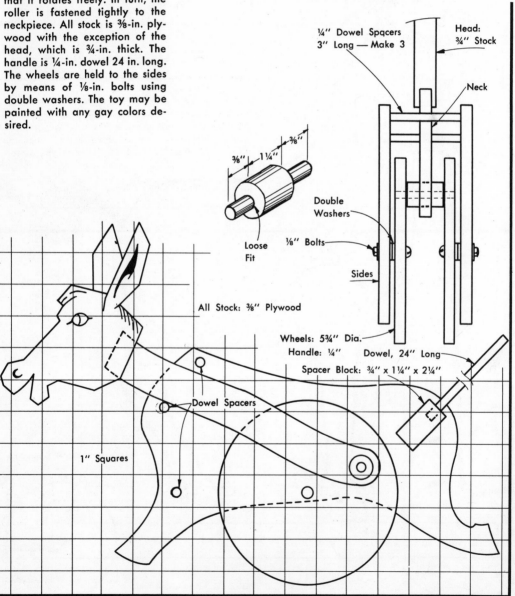

¼" Dowel Spacers
3" Long — Make 3

Head:
¾" Stock

Neck

⅜"   1¼"   ⅜"

⅜"

Double
Washers

Loose
Fit

⅛" Bolts

Sides

All Stock: ⅜" Plywood

Wheels: 5¾" Dia.

Handle: ¼"   Dowel, 24" Long

Spacer Block: ¾" x 1¼" x 2¼"

Dowel Spacers

1" Squares

SIMPLE TANK

This interesting toy has a minimum number of parts which are easily assembled. The body is cut out of a solid piece of pine. The wheels can be turned on a lathe but the most convenient method is to use a 1⅛-in. closet pole dowel, cut and center-drilled as explained in the section on Wheels at the front of the book. Drill the holes large enough so that the wheels turn freely on the screws. The turret is turned out of a piece of pine on the lathe. The cannon is a ⅜-in. dowel tapered to ¼ in. The assembled toy may be enameled or lacquered in olive green or gray.

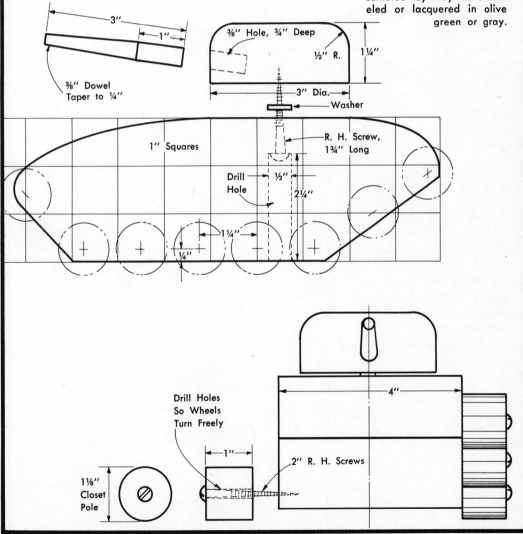

TOY TANK

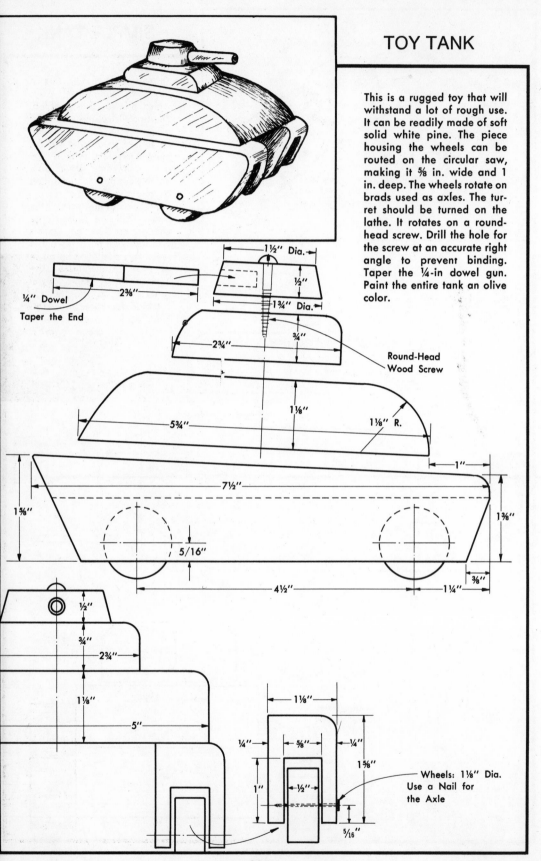

This is a rugged toy that will withstand a lot of rough use. It can be readily made of soft solid white pine. The piece housing the wheels can be routed on the circular saw, making it ⅝ in. wide and 1 in. deep. The wheels rotate on brads used as axles. The turret should be turned on the lathe. It rotates on a round-head screw. Drill the hole for the screw at an accurate right angle to prevent binding. Taper the ¼-in dowel gun. Paint the entire tank an olive color.

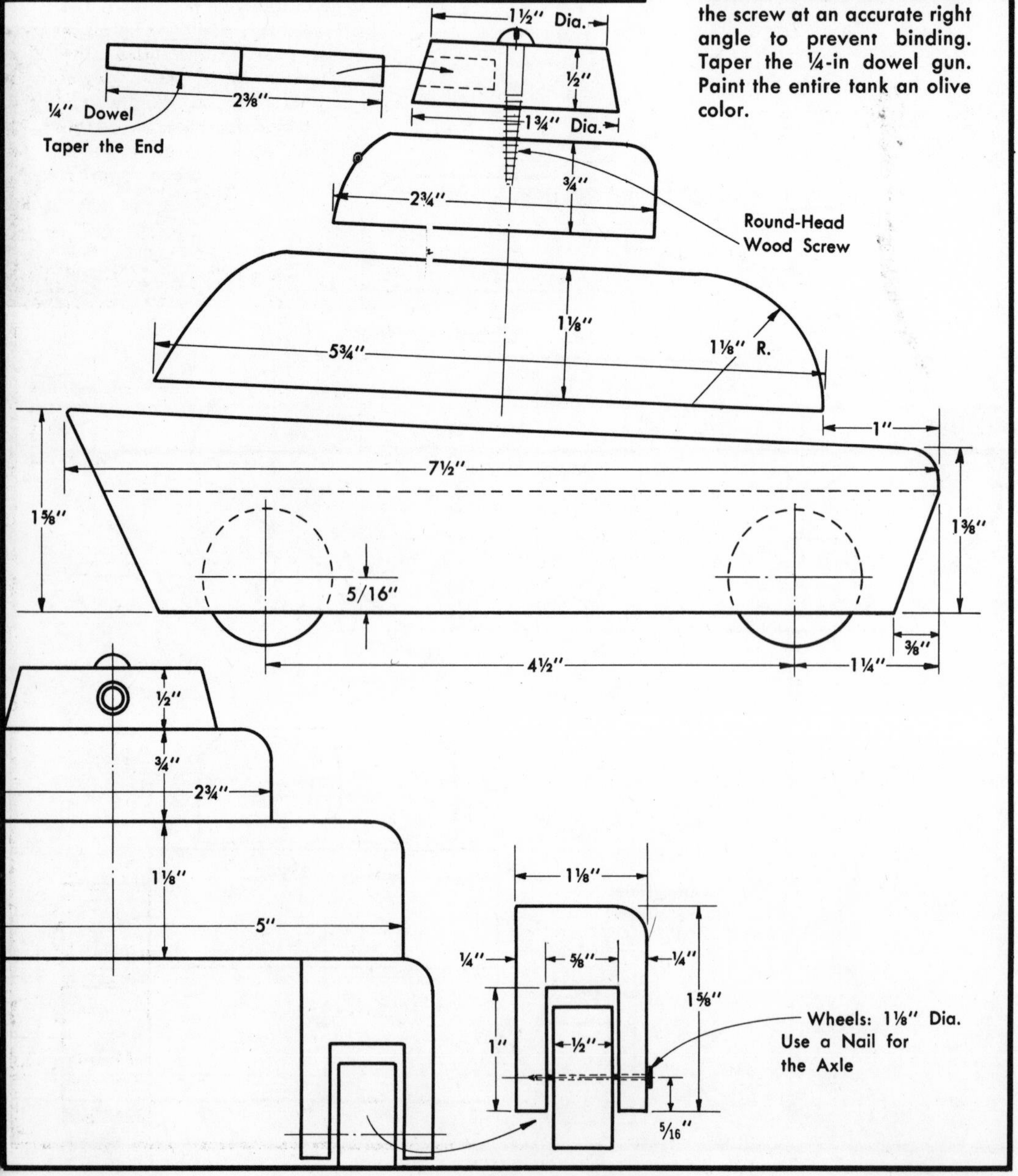
1½" Dia.
½"
1¾" Dia.
¼" Dowel
Taper the End
2⅜"
2¾"
¾"
Round-Head
Wood Screw
1⅛"
5¾"
1⅛" R.
1"
7½"
1⅝"
1⅜"
5/16"
⅜"
4½"
1¼"
½"
¾"
2¾"
1⅛"
5"
1⅛"
¼"
⅝"
¼"
1⅝"
1"
½"
Wheels: 1⅛" Dia.
Use a Nail for
the Axle
5/16"

HORSE AND WAGON

This is both a toy and a model, especially if care is taken with the details and if all the cuts are made accurately. Softwood such as basswood or soft, straight-grained pine, is best for this project. Do not use hard or grainy wood which is difficult to work. Cut a pair of wheels at the same time. The spokes can be cut; if plain disk wheels are used, spokes can be painted on them. The wheels are held in place with flat-headed nails. The wagon box should be made first. The axles are then made and nailed to the bottom of the box. Next, the shafts are made and nailed to the block on the front axle. The wheels can then be mounted. The outline of the horse is traced on ¾-in. stock and sawed out either with a jig saw or a coping saw. Tiny nails hold the horse in the shafts. The toy is finished in bright enamels.

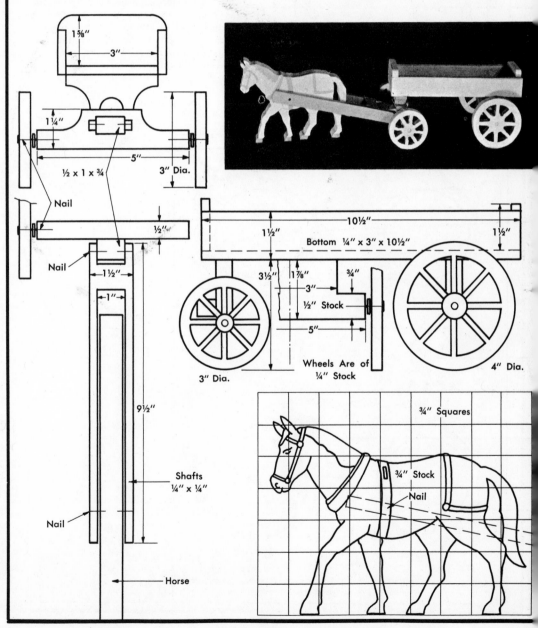

1⅝"
3"
1¼"
5"
½ x 1 x ¾
3" Dia.
Nail
½"
Nail
1½"
1"
9½"
Shafts ¼" x ¼"
Nail
Horse

10½"
1½"
1½"
Bottom ¼" x 3" x 10½"
3½"
1⅞"
¾"
3"
½" Stock
5"
3" Dia.
Wheels Are of ¼" Stock
4" Dia.

¾" Squares
¾" Stock
Nail

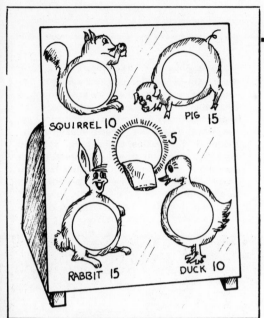

BEANBAG GAME

The game of beanbag is "as old as the hills" yet each new generation must be taught the delights of this amusing pastime. The board is simple to make. Use ¼-in. wallboard, or plywood if you desire, but the wallboard is better since it is simple to cut and decorate. Use a heavy 2 by 8-in. piece for the base to keep the board upright. Paint the board white with the figures in brown, red, orange, and blue.

Make three beanbags about 3 by 4 in. but do not fill them too tight. For added interest and practice in arithmetic, the bags can be of different colors with these scoring values: the blue bag rates the regular score as shown on the board, the red bag doubles the score, and the yellow bag triples the score.

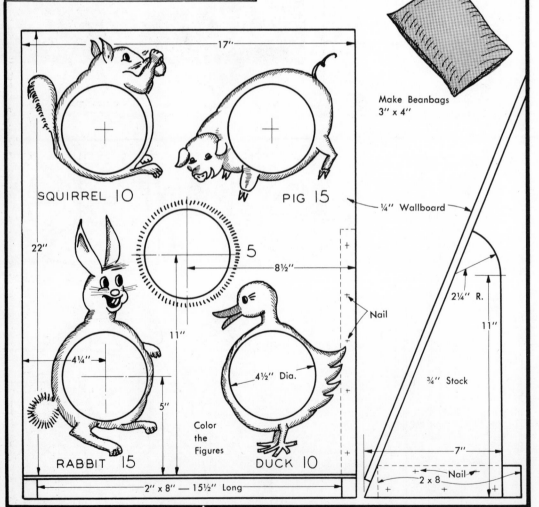

SQUIRREL 10

PIG 15

5

RABBIT 15

DUCK 10

Color the Figures

17"

22"

8½"

11"

4¼"

5"

4½" Dia.

Nail

2" x 8" — 15½" Long

Make Beanbags 3" x 4"

¼" Wallboard

2¼" R.

11"

¾" Stock

7"

2 x 8

Nail

This ring-toss game is fun and will test the skill of old and young alike. It is a lathe project.   The clowns and the ½ sphere bases may be made of any available wood. Note that the ¼-in. dowel extends 1 in. into the head, through the ½ sphere base and into the bottom board. Glue the assemblies together. The bottom board may be ½-in. plywood. Paint the faces white with the features in black and the hats and the bases in bright contrasting colors such as orange, blue, and green. The rings should be made of ¼-in. thick plywood or wallboard which is lighter in weight. Mark the silk hat figure 15, the middle one 10, and the pointed cap 5 for scoring.

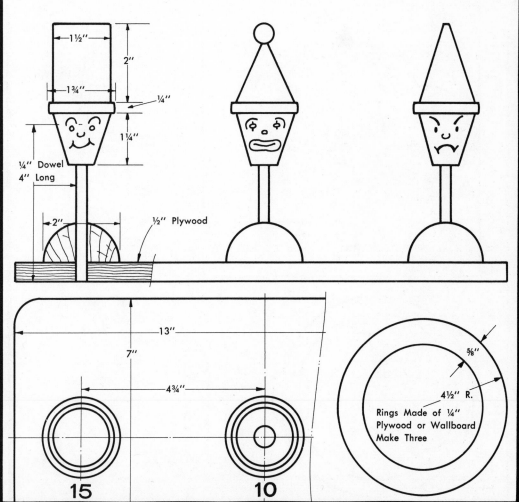

ROPE RING QUOITS

This is a game of skill that is easy to make using ½-in. plywood for the board and ½-in. dowels, spaced as shown. Paint the board as indicated. The quoits are made of ½-in. rope. Cut 16-in. lengths for as many as you want, although six are sufficient. The wooden joiners are made of 1-in. dowel, 1¼ in. long, drilled on the drill press. Bevel the holes for easy insertion of the rope. Wrap a few strands of string around the rope ends, coat the holes and rope ends with heavy glue, assemble, and allow to dry.

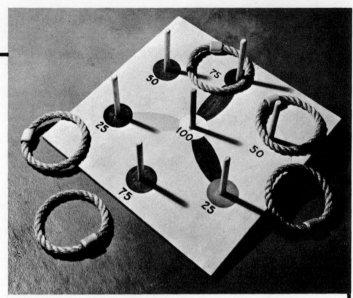

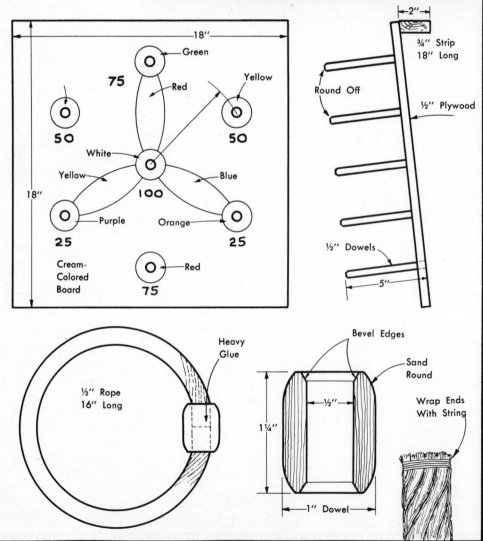

OPEN-SIDE DOLLHOUSE

There is nothing difficult about the construction of this attractive dollhouse. All eight pieces of ¼-in. plywood or wallboard may be cut out of a panel 3 by 4 ft. Nail together the two pieces of stock for the sides and then cut them at the same time. Cut the three floors and the three inside walls in the same manner. This method assures accuracy and facilitates assembly. Use heavy glue and nail together with 1-in. brads. First nail the back to the floors, then add the sides. The chimney is a 1 by 2-in. block of white pine with a ¼-in. cap. Paint the house in attractive colors both inside and out. The open side provides the young housekeeper with access to all the rooms.

Cut Roof Boards at These Angles

Chimney

5"

Inside Walls — Make Three

8¼"

6"

Sides — Make Two

6"

14¼"

12¾"

6"

8½"

2¼"

1¼"

¼"

⅛"

2"

1"

1¾"

Cut These Angles to Fit Roof

Chimney — Nail ¼" Cap Onto Solid Block

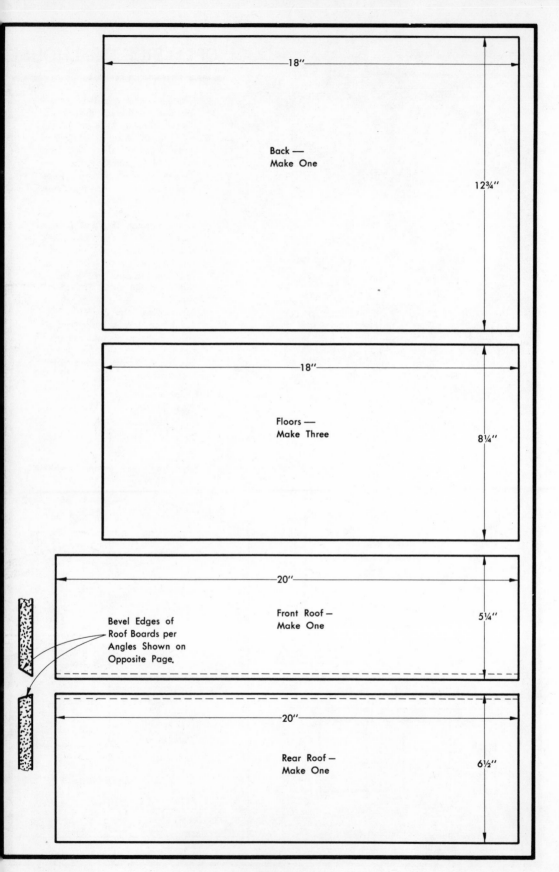

Back —
Make One

18″

12¾″

Floors —
Make Three

18″

8¼″

Front Roof —
Make One

20″

5¼″

Bevel Edges of
Roof Boards per
Angles Shown on
Opposite Page.

Rear Roof —
Make One

20″

6½″

DOLLHOUSE

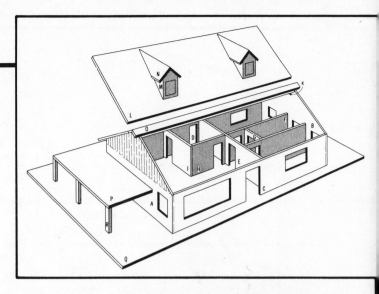

This attractive dollhouse will delight any little girl. It is large enough to accommodate quite a bit of furniture and the entire roof is removable to provide access to all the rooms. It is quite simple to build, with the use of either ¼-in. plywood or wallboard. Cut the ends A and B and the sides C and D at the same time so that they match. Glue and nail them to-

gether first, then add the ridge block K. Mount this assembly on the base Q and then add the inner walls. Now the roof and dormers may be added, after which the carport and porch are put in place. When assembling, use plenty of glue and flathead nails. Paint the house in suitable colors.

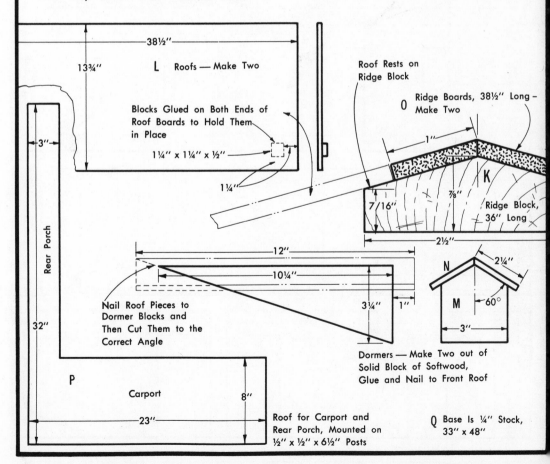

38½"

13¾"

L   Roofs — Make Two

Blocks Glued on Both Ends of Roof Boards to Hold Them in Place

1¼" x 1¼" x ½"

1¼"

Roof Rests on Ridge Block

Ridge Boards, 38½" Long — Make Two

0

1"

K

7/8"

7/16"

Ridge Block, 36" Long

2½"

3"

Rear Porch

12"

10¼"

Nail Roof Pieces to Dormer Blocks and Then Cut Them to the Correct Angle

3¼"   1"

2¼"

N

M   60°

3"

32"

Dormers — Make Two out of Solid Block of Softwood, Glue and Nail to Front Roof

P

Carport

8"

23"

Roof for Carport and Rear Porch, Mounted on ½" x ½" x 6½" Posts

Q   Base Is ¼" Stock, 33" x 48"

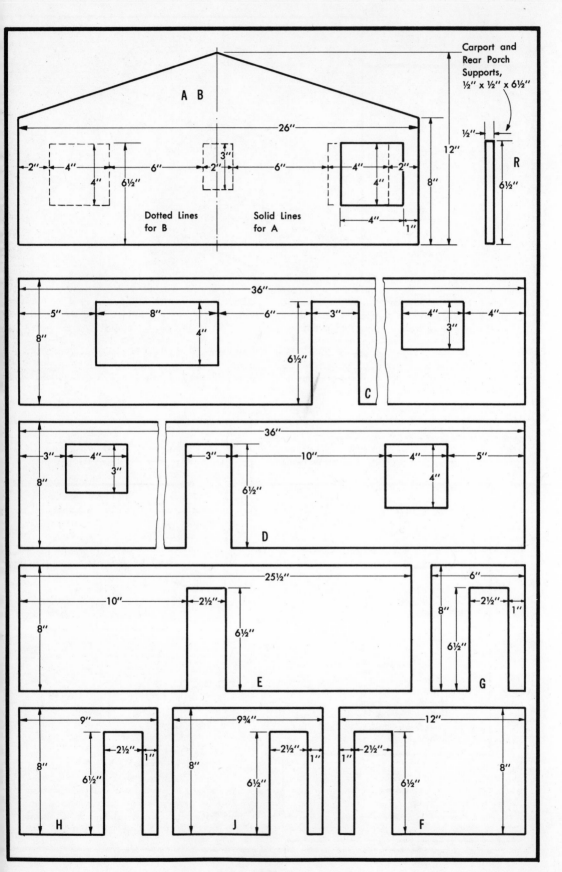

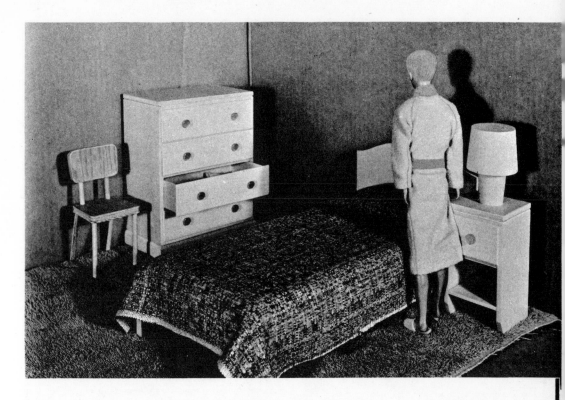

HIGH-FASHION DOLL FURNITURE

With the introduction of lifelike dolls of high-fashion style, little girls want scale furniture to go along with the many accessories available for these dolls. Typical of their wants is the letter to the right. The author wrote to one of his granddaughters telling her that he was designing and building this furniture and asked what she would like most. The reply is self-explanatory. The only difficult request is the "wall-to-wall carpeting" since the writer does not intend to build a house for these dolls. The reason: these dolls are about one-fifth actual size. Thus a 10 x 12-ft. bedroom would be 2 x 2½ ft. A 15 by 20-ft. living room would be 3 by 4 ft. — rather large for a dollhouse in today's homes!

Shown here are a number of pieces of furniture that will add to the children's fun when they play with these dolls. They are made to a scale of 3/16 in. to 1 in. For best results use basswood plywood, which can be obtained from such firms as Albert Constantine & Son, 2050 Eastchester Road, New York, N. Y. 10061, or Craftsman Wood Service, 2729 S. Mary Street, Chicago, Ill. 60608. With careful attention to accuracy and a little patience, delightful and realistic furniture can be made.

General Construction

For best results in making this doll furniture, use basswood plywood in ⅛-, 3/16-, and ¼-in.

Jan. 22

Dear Grandpa,
Thank you for the nice letter. I would like a closet, a bed, a mirror, a table, a night stand with lamp, cupbord, sink, a stove, couch, two lamps, a T.V, a picture frame, a coat hanger, wall to wall carpeting, a bathroom, a small rug

Thank you very much.

Love

Cindy

thicknesses. It can be obtained from the sources listed on the opposite page. If you have a circular saw, a hollow ground blade will enable you to make the parts with ease and accuracy. Accurcy is important in construction, so check and double check all cuts before they are made. The use of basswood plywood and a hollow-ground blade practically eliminates all sanding so that parts fit squarely. Assemble the parts with an adhesive such as Elmer's Glue and the finest wire brads you can buy in ⅜- and ½-in. lengths.

When making several pieces of the same size, cut them to rough dimensions, use fine brads to hold the pieces together, and then cut the parts at the same time. This assures complete accuracy. The horizontal spacers in the dresser are an example. If you cut all of these pieces at the same time, there is no chance of error or misfit. When making a number of chairs, use can be made of a drill press with a little jig to hold the part when drilling. This will speed up the operation and again result in uniform parts that will insure accurate fit and alignment. When cutting the dowel legs, use a stop on the band saw

or circular saw or use a miter box if they are cut by hand. This will assure uniform lengths.

In making any item of furniture that has drawers, it is best to make the drawers first and then the rest of the piece. By following this procedure you can be sure that the drawers will fit perfectly and operate smoothly.

In finishing, use 00 sandpaper. A light-colored stain such as blonde or ash and a final coat of brushing lacquer are recommended. Consult your local paint store regarding the stain and finish.

Drawer Construction

At first, the construction of the drawers for this doll furniture may seem difficult but it is quite simple if they are made with care and accuracy. The trick is to make all similar parts at the same time. Thus, if four drawers are required for the dresser, make the four bottoms, fronts, backs, and eight sides with the same setup so they will all have the same dimensions. Since the fronts, bottoms, and backs are of the same width, they may be cut from the same piece (**D, B** and **F**) to the proper lengths. This assures perfect assembly. Use ¼-in. brads and glue. The front face is a separate ⅛-in. piece which is glued to the front of the box drawer. The knobs are 5/16-in.-diameter plastic dress buttons available at any variety store. Drill a fine hole in the stem of the button and a similar hole in the drawer front. Cut off a small wire nail, insert it from the inside of the drawer through the front, and apply ambroid cement to the button and nail to secure it in place.

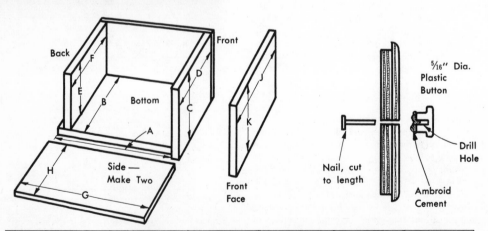

Furniture	Bottom 3/16" Stock		Front 3/16" Stock		Back 3/16" Stock		Sides ⅛" Stock		Front Face ⅛" Stock	
	A	B	C	D	E	F	G	H	J	K
Night Stand (1)	2⅛	2⅜	1½	2⅜	1 3/16	2⅜	2⅜	1½	2⅝	1¾
Dresser (3)	3 9/16	8⅛	1½	8⅛	1⅛	8⅛	3¾	1½	8½	1¾
Chest of Drawers (4)	3 7/16	6	1½	6	1⅛	6	3⅝	1½	6½	1¾

CHEST OF DRAWERS

General construction suggestions and detail drawer dimensions have already been presented. Make the four drawers first and then construct the unit shown here. In this way you will be certain that the drawers will fit accurately. First nail and glue the sidepieces to the shelf dividers. Then nail this assembly to the ¾-in. base block. Now glue on the top, nailing it from below and then glue the cardboard back into place. The heavy, solid ¾-in. base adds weight so that the drawers may be opened and closed without tipping the unit. Finish with a light-colored stain and dull varnish or lacquer.

Bill of Materials

Sides (Two)	¼" x 3⅞" x 7½"
Dividers (Five)	¼" x 3¾" x 6 5/16"
Top (One)	¼" x 3⅞" x 6 13/16"
Base (One)	¾" x 4" x 7"

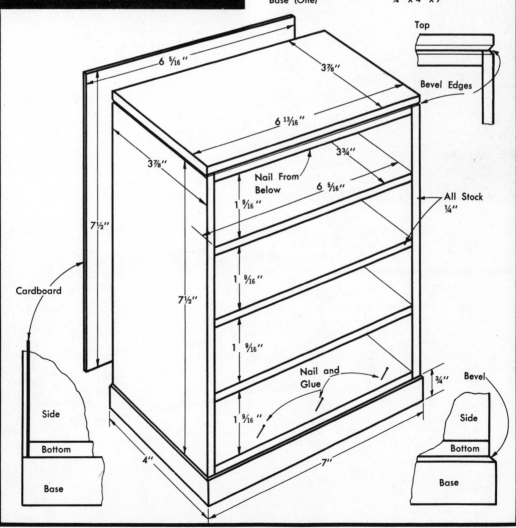

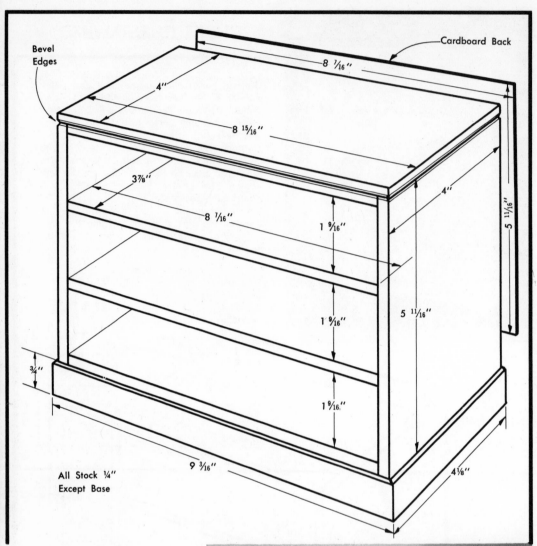

Bevel
Edges

Cardboard Back

8 7/16"

4"

8 15/16"

3 7/8"

8 7/16"

4"

5 11/16"

1 9/16"

5 11/16"

1 9/16"

3/4"

1 9/16"

All Stock 1/4"
Except Base

9 3/16"

4 1/8"

DRESSER

The construction of this
dresser is the same as that of
the chest of drawers shown
on the opposite page. The
drawer dimensions and their
construction are shown on a
preceding page.

Bill of Materials

Sides (Two)	1/4" x 4" x 5 11/16"
Dividers (Four)	1/4" x 3 7/8" x 8 7/16"
Top (One)	1/4" x 4" x 8 15/16"
Base (One)	3/4" x 4 1/8" x 9 3/16"

NIGHTSTAND AND LAMP

The general construction and the details of how the drawer is made including drawer dimensions are given on a preceding page. The use of basswood plywood will simplify construction and be an aid to accurate work. All parts are ¼ in. thick except the lower shelf which is 3/16 in. Cut the divider shelves and the lower shelf at the same time. Then cut the sides and assemble them with the shelves, using glue and thin wire brads. The last operation is gluing the top in place after the edges have been beveled as indicated. Finish with a light-colored stain and flat varnish or lacquer.

Sides (Two)	¼" x 2⅝" x 5"
Dividers (Two)	¼" x 2⅝" x 2 9/16"
Shelf (One)	3/16" x 2⅝" x 2 9/16"
Top (One)	¼" x 2⅝" x 3 1/16"

THE LAMP

This is a lathe project which can easily be turned out of white pine or other softwood. Sand it smooth. Paint the shade a light cream color and the base a darker color.

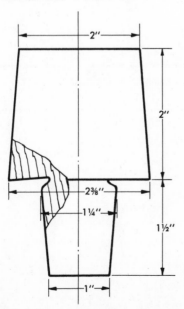

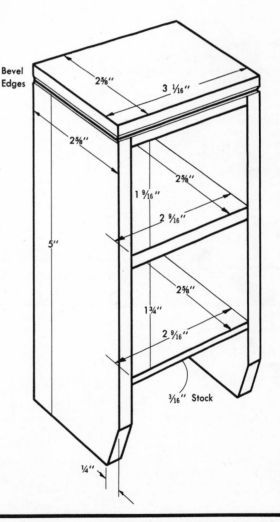

49

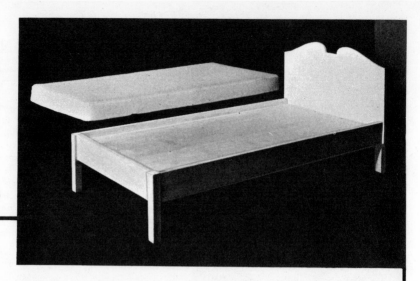

TWIN BEDS

The detail drawings show how these beds are to be constructed. Make two of them. Use basswood plywood for all parts except the legs, which may be soft white pine. Make the headboard first and then the footboard; then nail and glue on the side rails. Fit in the 1/8-in. bottom board and nail and glue it to the end cleats. Put in glue blocks along the inside of the side rails to support the bottom. The mattress is a piece of foam upholstery material obtainable as scrap in any upholstery shop.

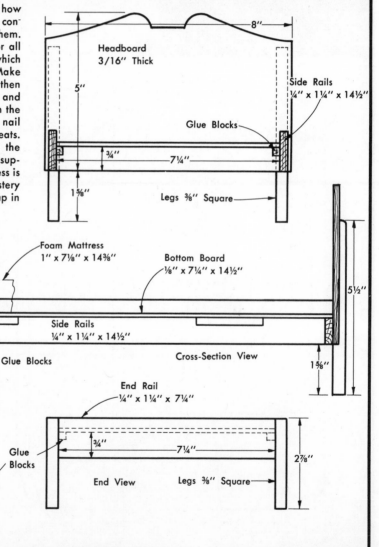

Headboard 3/16" Thick

8"

5"

Side Rails 1/4" x 1 1/4" x 14 1/2"

Glue Blocks

3/4"

7 1/4"

1 5/8"

Legs 3/8" Square

Foam Mattress 1" x 7 1/8" x 14 3/8"

Bottom Board 1/8" x 7 1/4" x 14 1/2"

5 1/2"

Side Rails 1/4" x 1 1/4" x 14 1/2"

3/8"

Glue Blocks

Cross-Section View

1 5/8"

End Rail 1/4" x 1 1/4" x 7 1/4"

End Cleats 3/8" x 3/4" x 7 1/4"

Glue Blocks

3/4"

7 1/4"

2 7/8"

Top View

End View

Legs 3/8" Square

50

DINING-ROOM TABLE

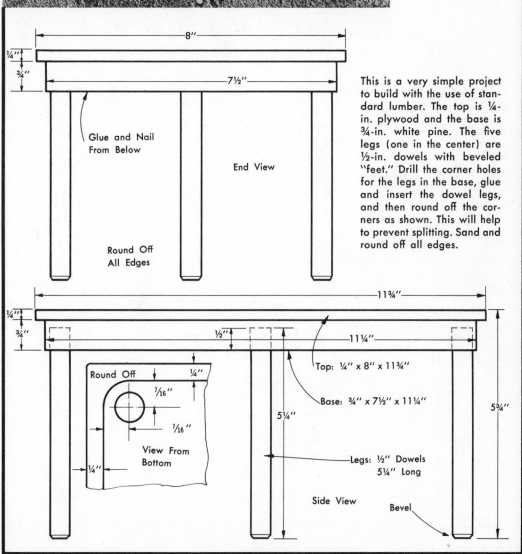

8"

¼"

¾"

7½"

Glue and Nail
From Below

End View

Round Off
All Edges

This is a very simple project to build with the use of standard lumber. The top is ¼-in. plywood and the base is ¾-in. white pine. The five legs (one in the center) are ½-in. dowels with beveled "feet." Drill the corner holes for the legs in the base, glue and insert the dowel legs, and then round off the corners as shown. This will help to prevent splitting. Sand and round off all edges.

11¾"

¼"

¾"

½"

11¼"

Round Off

¼"

7/16"

7/16"

¼"

View From
Bottom

5¼"

Top: ¼" x 8" x 11¾"

Base: ¾" x 7½" x 11¼"

5¾"

Legs: ½" Dowels
5¼" Long

Side View

Bevel

CHAIRS

Of all the pieces of doll furniture, the chairs are perhaps the most appealing and attractive. At the same time, a chair is the most difficult to make. However, if care is taken in cutting the parts and you have a drill press, construction will be greatly simplified. First cut the seat and the parts for the backrest. To assure that the seat parts and leg spacing will be uniform, make an accurate template out of metal from a "tin-can" or an aluminum offset plate with pin-holes at the centers where each hole is to be drilled. Mark each seat and drill the holes at the angles **A** and **B** as shown as well as right angles for the front legs. You can make a little wooden jig to hold each part in place on the drill press so that they will all be uniform. After the seat is drilled, the remaining operations are simple. Cut the dowels and assemble the parts with glue, using short, cutoff brads to nail the uprights to the backrest. Bevel the legs at the bottom and smooth and round off all edges.

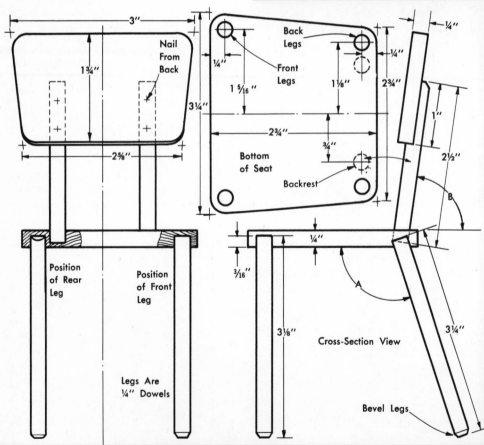

3"

1¾"

Nail From Back

2⅝"

Position of Rear Leg

Position of Front Leg

Legs Are ¼" Dowels

Back Legs

Front Legs

¼"

1 5/16"

2¾"

¾"

Bottom of Seat

Backrest

1⅛"

¼"

3¼"

¼"

¼"

2¾"

1"

2½"

B

A

3/16"

¼"

3⅛"

Cross-Section View

3¼"

Bevel Legs

52

FOLDING IRONING BOARD

The dimensions of the legs of this ironing board must be accurately adhered to so that they will fold compactly with the proper clearance. The legs are made of ¾ by 1¼-in. white pine. The top, which should be padded after assembly, is made of ½-in. plywood. The cross members of the leg assemblies are ½-in. dowels with the exception of the top, inner leg unit, which is a ¾ by 1-in. block, 4½ in. long. This miniature ironing board has exceptional rigidity and will afford many hours of realistic play.

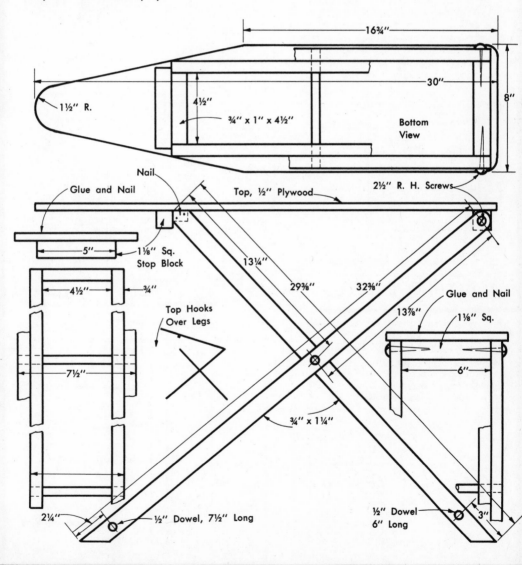

16¾"

30"

8"

1½" R.

4½"

¾" x 1" x 4½"

Bottom View

2½" R. H. Screws

Nail

Glue and Nail

Top, ½" Plywood

5"

1⅛" Sq. Stop Block

13¼"

4½"

¾"

Top Hooks Over Legs

29⅜"

32⅜"

Glue and Nail

13⅞"

1⅛" Sq.

7½"

6"

¾" x 1¼"

2¼"

½" Dowel, 7½" Long

½" Dowel 6" Long

3"

SPINNER TOP

This is an ideal lathe project. Make the top out of hardwood for greater weight so it spins longer. For perfect balance follow Steps 1, 2, and 3 as shown below. Put a brass round-headed nail in the point of the top to reduce friction. The handle may be made of pine. Use a 26-in. shoelace for winding the top.

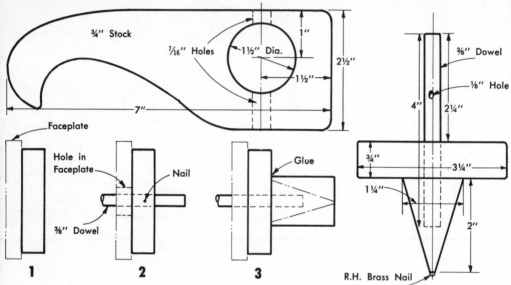

¾" Stock
7/16" Holes
1½" Dia.
1"
2½"
1½"
7"

Faceplate

Hole in Faceplate
Nail
⅜" Dowel

Glue

⅜" Dowel
⅛" Hole
4"
2¼"
¾"
3¼"
1¼"
2"
R.H. Brass Nail

1 **2** **3**

AERO PROPELLER

This toy provides great fun for out-of-doors since, if used inside, it has such force and rises so rapidly it could mar the ceiling. Make the propeller out of the metal from a tin can or lightweight aluminum and shape the wings as indicated with the ends bent up.

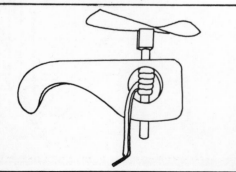

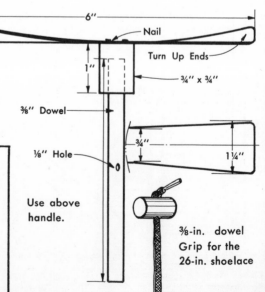

6"
Nail
Turn Up Ends
1"
¾" x ¾"
⅜" Dowel
⅛" Hole
¾"
1¼"

Use above handle.

⅜-in. dowel
Grip for the 26-in. shoelace

TRIPLE WINDMILL

To reduce friction, use bushings made of brass tubing as shown below. Select the tubing that will fit the screws you use, and then drill holes in the propellers and the main pivot to hold the bushings tight. Use roundheaded screws at least 3½ in. long for the large propeller and main pivot, and 2-in. screws for the two smaller propellers. The tail is made of lightweight aluminum inserted in a fine saw cut in the horizontal main body. Locate the main pivot (X) by balancing the entire windmill after assembly. Paint the entire unit white.

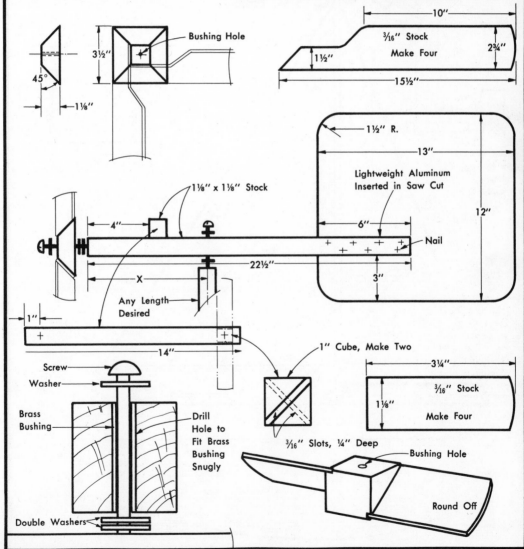

45°
1⅛"
3½"
Bushing Hole

10"
³⁄₁₆" Stock
Make Four
1½"
2¾"
15½"

1½" R.
13"
Lightweight Aluminum Inserted in Saw Cut
12"
6"
Nail
3"

1⅛" x 1⅛" Stock
4"
22½"
X
Any Length Desired
1"
14"

Screw
Washer
Brass Bushing
Drill Hole to Fit Brass Bushing Snugly
Double Washers

1" Cube, Make Two
³⁄₁₆" Slots, ¼" Deep

3¼"
³⁄₁₆" Stock
Make Four
1⅛"

Bushing Hole
Round Off

SAIL, HO!

If you start early enough, this can be a one-evening project since it is so simple to build. Use white pine for the boat and ¼-in. dowels for the mast and spar. Install the tiller through the hole in the boat and then solder on the rudder. The sails may be made of white cotton. The model shown has sails made of thin plastic from an old raincoat and the existing hems were used. Paint the boat white with a green top and an orange deck.

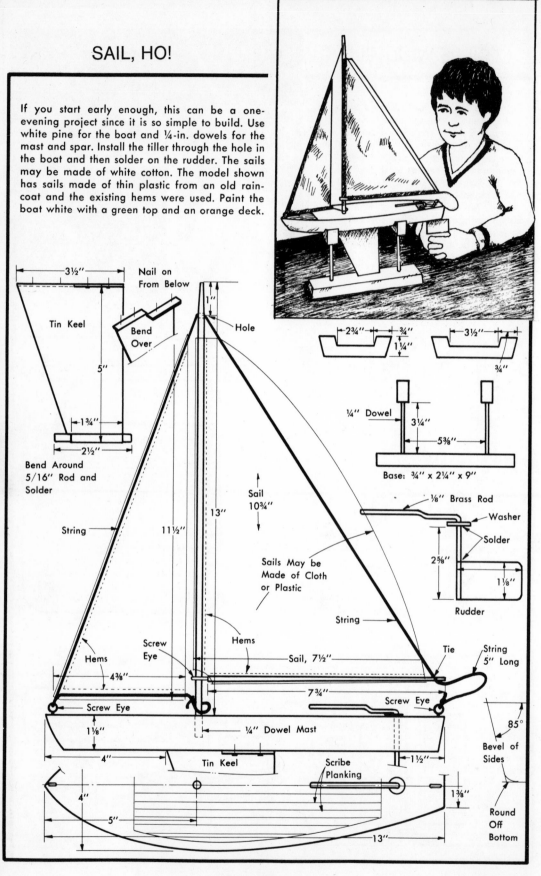

3½"

Tin Keel

Nail on From Below

Bend Over

Hole

1"

5"

1¾"

2½"

Bend Around 5/16" Rod and Solder

String

13"

11½"

Sail 10¾"

Sails May be Made of Cloth or Plastic

2¾"   ¾"   1¼"

3½"   ¾"

¼" Dowel

3¼"

5⅜"

Base: ¾" x 2¼" x 9"

⅛" Brass Rod

Washer

Solder

2⅝"

1⅛"

Rudder

String

Hems

Screw Eye

Hems

4⅜"

Sail, 7½"

String

Tie

String 5" Long

Screw Eye

Screw Eye

7¾"

1⅛"

¼" Dowel Mast

Tin Keel

Scribe Planking

1½"

85°

Bevel of Sides

4"

4"

5"

13"

1⅜"

Round Off Bottom

56

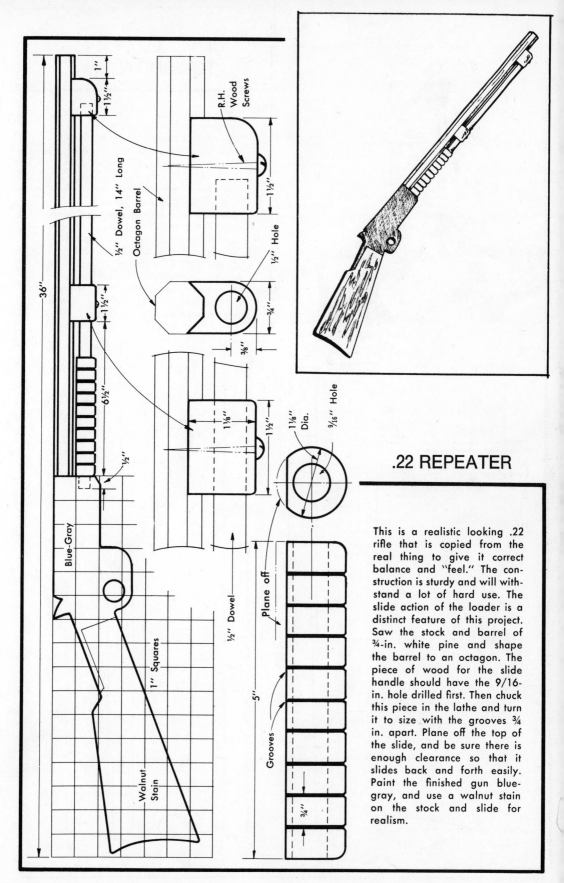

.22 REPEATER

This is a realistic looking .22 rifle that is copied from the real thing to give it correct balance and "feel." The construction is sturdy and will withstand a lot of hard use. The slide action of the loader is a distinct feature of this project. Saw the stock and barrel of ¾-in. white pine and shape the barrel to an octagon. The piece of wood for the slide handle should have the 9/16-in. hole drilled first. Then chuck this piece in the lathe and turn it to size with the grooves ¾ in. apart. Plane off the top of the slide, and be sure there is enough clearance so that it slides back and forth easily. Paint the finished gun blue-gray, and use a walnut stain on the stock and slide for realism.

Diagram labels:
36"
1"
1½"
R.H. Wood Screws
½" Dowel, 14" Long
Octagon Barrel
½" Hole
1½"
6½"
¾"
⅜"
½"
1⅛"
1½"
1⅛" Dia.
9/16" Hole
Blue-Gray
1" Squares
Walnut Stain
5"
½" Dowel
Plane off
Grooves
¾"

TOY SHOTGUN

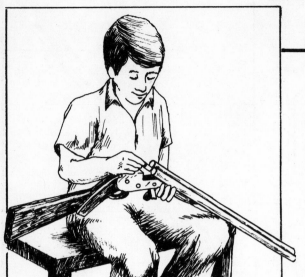

This toy gun is so realistic it has fooled many an adult. The stock is made of 1⅛-in. white pine with a carved handle grip. The side plates are made of ⅜-in. stock. The hand grip below the barrels is also 1⅛-in. pine. The barrels are 1-in. dowels with the ends bored ¾ in. in diameter and 2 in. deep for shells. The shells are ¾-in.-diameter dowels. Paint them red and black. The gun "breaks" by means of a dowel at the hinge. Cut a groove in each end of the dowel to make it look like a screw. Paint the gun blue-black; use walnut stain on the stock. This toy is a good means of teaching youngsters how to handle a gun correctly.

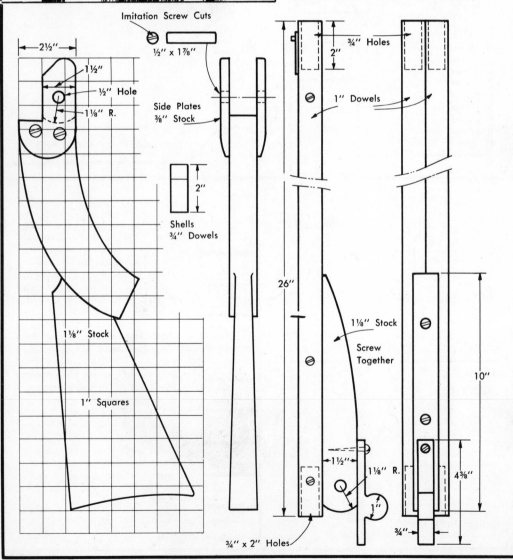

Imitation Screw Cuts

½" x 1⅞"

Side Plates ⅜" Stock

Shells ¾" Dowels

2½"

1½"

½" Hole

1⅛" R.

1⅛" Stock

1" Squares

2"

¾" Holes

2"

1" Dowels

26"

1⅛" Stock

Screw Together

10"

1½"

1⅛" R.

1"

4⅜"

¾"

¾" x 2" Holes

GARAGE

This garage is fun to build and fun to play with. Make it of ¼-in. plywood throughout, except the doors for which ⅜-in. stock is used. Glue and nail all pieces together. Cut two pieces, one for the back and the other for the front in which the door opening is cut. The windowsills and trim may be nailed in place before assembly. Paint the garage any pleasing color with contrasting trim.

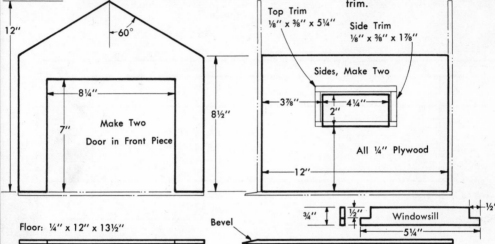

12"

60°

8¼"

7"

Make Two
Door in Front Piece

8½"

Top Trim
⅛" x ⅜" x 5¼"

Side Trim
⅛" x ⅜" x 1⅞"

Sides, Make Two

3⅞"

4¼"

2"

12"

All ¼" Plywood

Floor: ¼" x 12" x 13½"

Bevel

¾"

½"

Windowsill

5¼"

½"

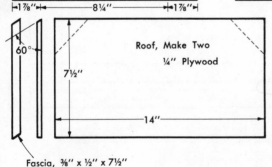

1⅞"

8¼"

1⅞"

60°

Roof, Make Two
¼" Plywood

7½"

14"

Fascia, ⅜" x ½" x 7½"

The garage shown has a hip roof at both ends which is more complicated to make than the plain gable roof. The hip may be made by cutting off the corners of the roof boards after assembly and then fitting and nailing a ¼-in. piece in place. The projecting corners of the ¼-in. piece should be trimmed to fit after it is in place.

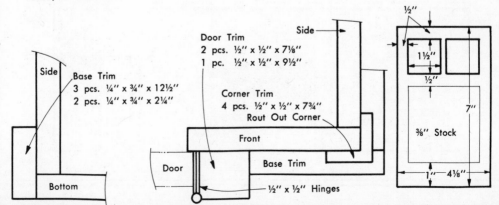

Side

Base Trim
3 pcs. ¼" x ¾" x 12½"
2 pcs. ¼" x ¾" x 2¼"

Bottom

Door Trim
2 pcs. ½" x ½" x 7⅛"
1 pc. ½" x ½" x 9½"

Corner Trim
4 pcs. ½" x ½" x 7¾"
Rout Out Corner

Front

Door

Base Trim

½" x ½" Hinges

Side

½"

1½"

½"

7"

⅜" Stock

1"

4⅛"

BARN

Use 3/16-in. wallboard for the main part of the barn. Assemble using heavy glue liberally and ¾-in. flat-headed nails. The use of glue blocks as indicated adds rigidity to the entire project. Paint the barn red with white trim. Paint the roof blue and the silo a mottled gray with a silver dome.

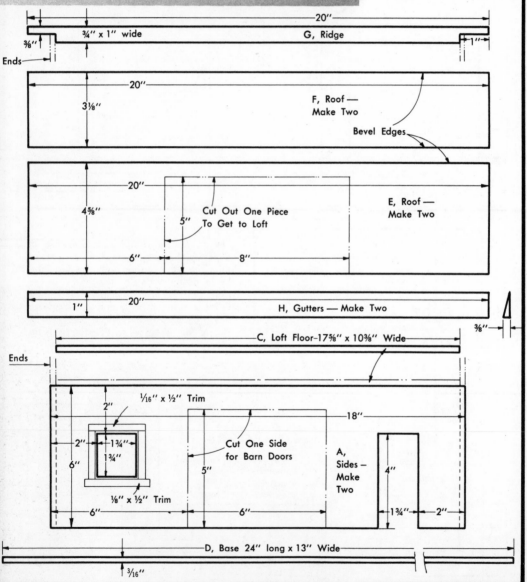

20"

¾" x 1" wide   G, Ridge   1"

⅜"

Ends

20"

3⅛"   F, Roof — Make Two

Bevel Edges

20"

4⅝"   Cut Out One Piece To Get to Loft   E, Roof — Make Two

5"

6"   8"

1"   20"   H, Gutters — Make Two

⅜"

C, Loft Floor-17⅝" x 10⅜" Wide

Ends

1/16" x ½" Trim

2"   18"

2"   1¾"   Cut One Side for Barn Doors   A, Sides — Make Two   4"

6"   1¾"

5"

⅛" x ½" Trim   1¾"   2"

6"   6"

D, Base 24" long x 13" Wide

3/16"

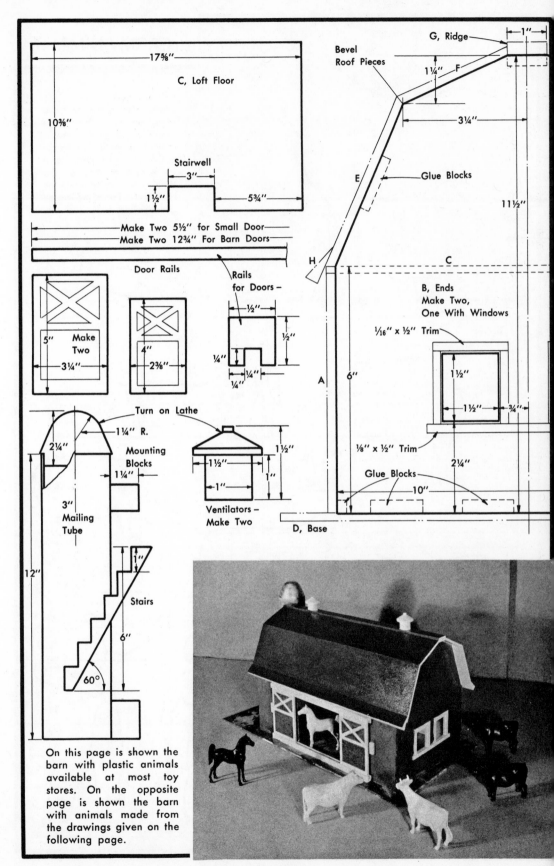

17⅝"

C, Loft Floor

10⅜"

Stairwell

3"

1½"

5¾"

Make Two 5½" for Small Door
Make Two 12¾" For Barn Doors

Door Rails

Rails for Doors –

½"

½"

¼"

¼"

¼"

5"

Make Two

3¼"

Make Two

4"

2⅜"

Turn on Lathe

1¼" R.

Mounting Blocks

1¼"

2¼"

3" Mailing Tube

12"

Stairs

1"

6"

60°

1½"

1"

1½"

1"

Ventilators – Make Two

G, Ridge

1"

Bevel Roof Pieces

1¼"

F

3¼"

E

Glue Blocks

11½"

H

C

B, Ends
Make Two,
One With Windows

1/16" x ½" Trim

1½"

1½"

¾"

A

6"

⅛" x ½" Trim

2¼"

Glue Blocks

10"

D, Base

On this page is shown the barn with plastic animals available at most toy stores. On the opposite page is shown the barn with animals made from the drawings given on the following page.

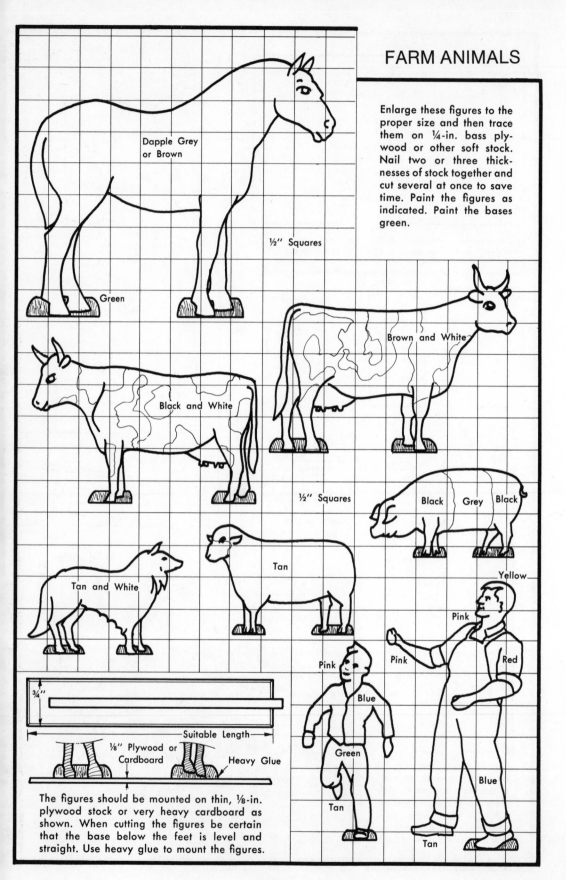

FARM ANIMALS

Enlarge these figures to the proper size and then trace them on ¼-in. bass plywood or other soft stock. Nail two or three thicknesses of stock together and cut several at once to save time. Paint the figures as indicated. Paint the bases green.

Dapple Grey or Brown

½" Squares

Green

Brown and White

Black and White

½" Squares

Black | Grey | Black

Tan and White

Tan

Yellow

Pink

Pink

Pink

Red

Blue

Pink

Green

Blue

Tan

¾"

Suitable Length

⅛" Plywood or Cardboard

Heavy Glue

Tan

The figures should be mounted on thin, ⅛-in. plywood stock or very heavy cardboard as shown. When cutting the figures be certain that the base below the feet is level and straight. Use heavy glue to mount the figures.

WORKBENCH

The construction of this workbench is so simple that little time is required to build it. Use ¾-in. pine throughout except for the top, which is ¼-in. plywood. Screw and glue all joints for greater strength and rigidity. Before assembling the parts, round off all edges and corners and sand them smooth. The completed unit may be given a stain and lacquer finish for permanence.

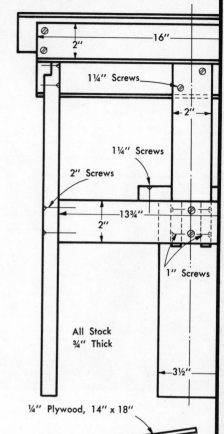

16"
2"
1¼" Screws
2"
1¼" Screws
2" Screws
13¾"
2"
1" Screws
All Stock ¾" Thick
3½"

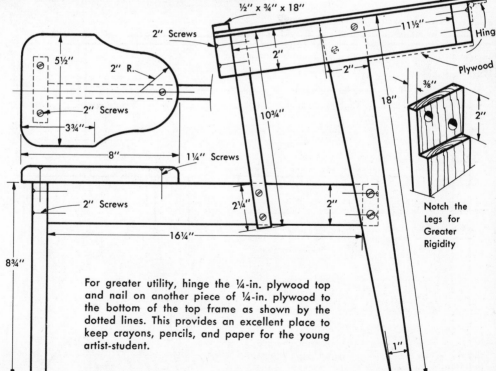

¼" Plywood, 14" x 18"
½" x ¾" x 18"
2" Screws
5½"
2" R.
2" Screws
3¾"
8"
1¼" Screws
2" Screws
16¼"
8¾"
2¼"
2"
11½"
2"
2"
10¾"
18"
Hinge
Plywood
⅜"
2"
Notch the Legs for Greater Rigidity
1"

For greater utility, hinge the ¼-in. plywood top and nail on another piece of ¼-in. plywood to the bottom of the top frame as shown by the dotted lines. This provides an excellent place to keep crayons, pencils, and paper for the young artist-student.

TABLE AND BENCHES

Not only will children get a lot of use out of this furniture but Mother and Dad, too, will use the little benches as footstools for reaching up to that high shelf. Use ½-in. plywood for all parts except the table legs, bench legs, and bench braces. Cut the pieces accurately so they can be glued and nailed together. Finish with clear lacquer and several coats of good wax. Decals may be added for decoration before the finish is applied. Round off the table legs as well as the bench tops.

BILL OF MATERIALS

Table

1	Top	½" x 19" x 28"
4	Legs	1¼" x 1¼" x 21"
2	Side Rails	½" x 3¾" x 25"
2	End Rails	½" x 3¾" x 17"

Benches — Two

2	Tops	½" x 9½" x 17"
4	Legs	¾" x 11½" x 13"
4	Side Rails	½" x 2¼" x 16"
2	Braces	¾" x 3½" x 14"

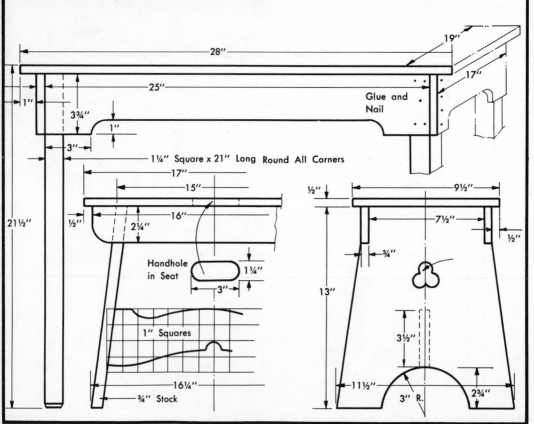

TABLE AND STOOLS

Designed for the young executive, here is a desk with a drawer that opens to both sides to store his crayons, paper, and pencils. There are also two lightweight, safe stools with hand holes for easy moving. The legs are tapered with beveled edges and have a ¾-in. turned dowel on one end for simple assembly. To obtain the correct angle for all of the legs, drill ¾-in. holes at the angle given on a 45-deg. line drawn from the corners of the tabletop and seats as shown. Drill the holes from below. Use white pine throughout and finish in clear lacquer or varnish.

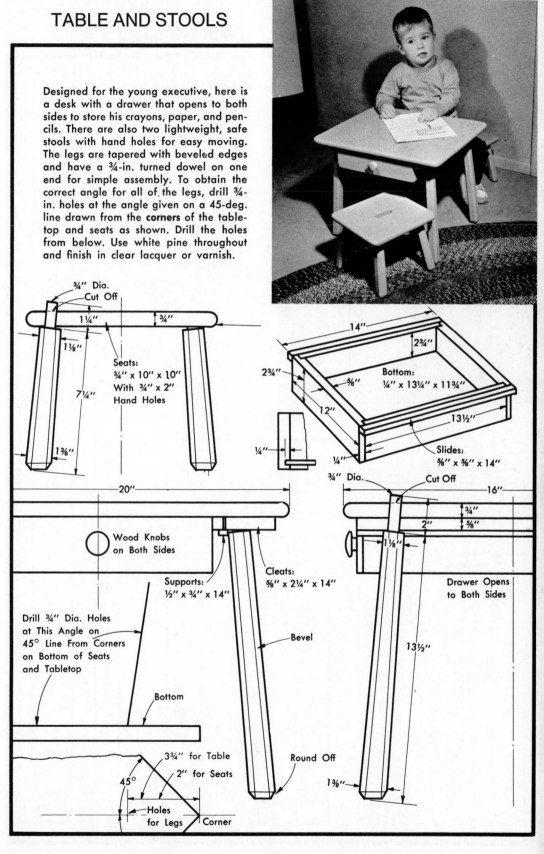

¾" Dia.
Cut Off
1¼"
¾"
1⅛"
Seats:
¾" x 10" x 10"
With ¾" x 2"
Hand Holes
7¼"
1⅜"

14"
2¾"
2¾"
⅝"
Bottom:
¼" x 13¼" x 11¾"
12"
13½"
¼"
¼"
Slides:
⅝" x ⅝" x 14"

¾" Dia.
Cut Off
16"
¾"
2"
⅝"
1⅛"
Drawer Opens
to Both Sides
13½"
1⅜"

20"
Wood Knobs
on Both Sides
Supports:
½" x ¾" x 14"
Cleats:
⅝" x 2¼" x 14"

Drill ¾" Dia. Holes
at This Angle on
45° Line From Corners
on Bottom of Seats
and Tabletop

Bevel

Round Off

Bottom

45°
3¾" for Table
2" for Seats
Holes
for Legs   Corner

WALKING STILTS

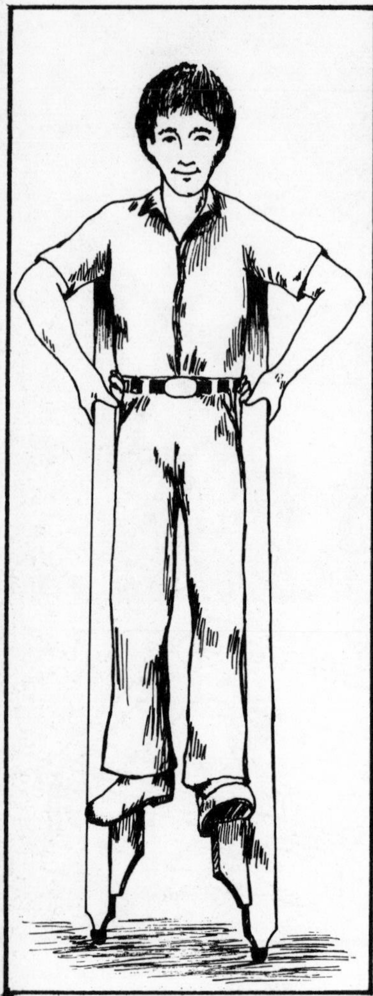

All boys (and some girls too) enjoy walking on stilts. It takes a little bit of practice to master them, which the youngsters easily accomplish. The two uprights are made of straight-grain white pine, tapered at the lower ends to accommodate 1-in. rubber crutch tips which keep the stilts from slipping. Drill the ⅜-in. holes accurately to center the bolts for the steps. The steps are also made of 1⅛-in. white pine with ⅜-in. plywood side guides which keep the steps upright. The steps are secured to the uprights by means of ⅜ x 5½-in. carriage bolts with wing nuts and washers. Round off and sand all edges and corners.

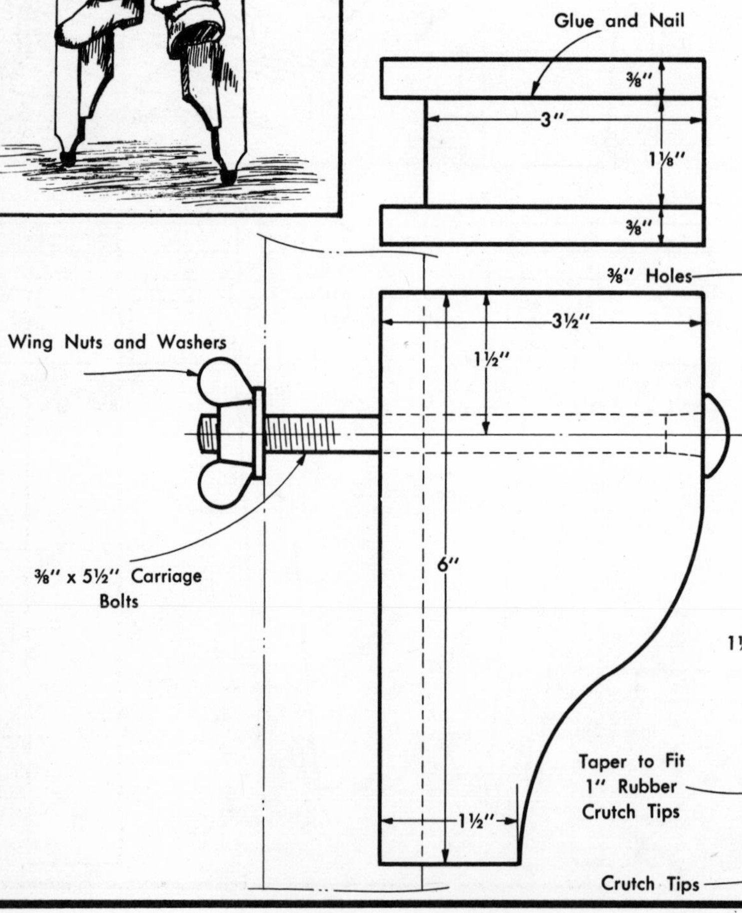
Glue and Nail
⅜″
3″
1⅛″
⅜″
3½″
1½″
Wing Nuts and Washers
⅜″ x 5½″ Carriage Bolts
6″
1½″

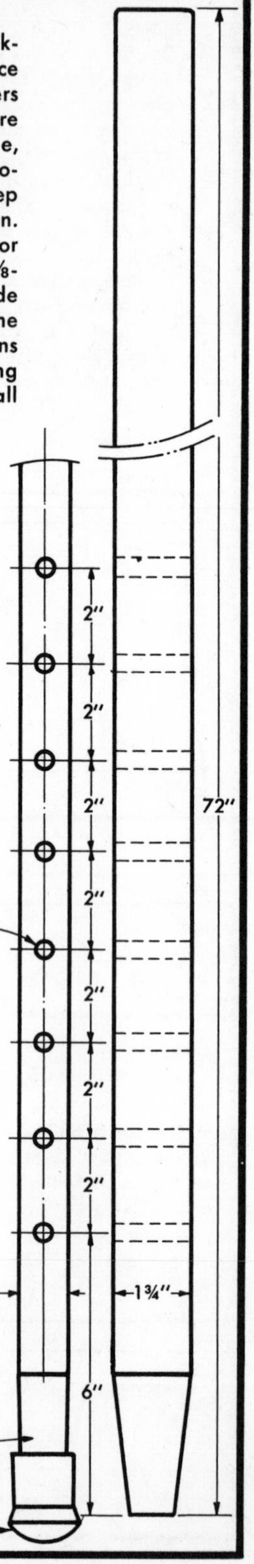
2″
2″
2″
2″
2″
2″
2″
72″
⅜″ Holes
1⅛″
1¾″
6″
Taper to Fit 1″ Rubber Crutch Tips
Crutch Tips

PEDAL CYCLE

The Pedal-Cycle is not difficult to make but it does take a bit of practice to learn how to use it. It is based on the principle of the unicycle and may be pedaled forward or backward as desired. The disks are best made of 1-in.-thick plywood or solid hardwood. Make three — two outside disks with one hole each, and one center disk with two holes as shown. Drill the holes for the ½-in. dowels accurately for a tight fit — they may not wobble. Secure the dowels by nailing. Be sure to slip the pieces of ⅝-in. conduit over the dowels before assembly. They act as rollers. The entire unit may be decorated if desired and given a coat of varnish or lacquer.

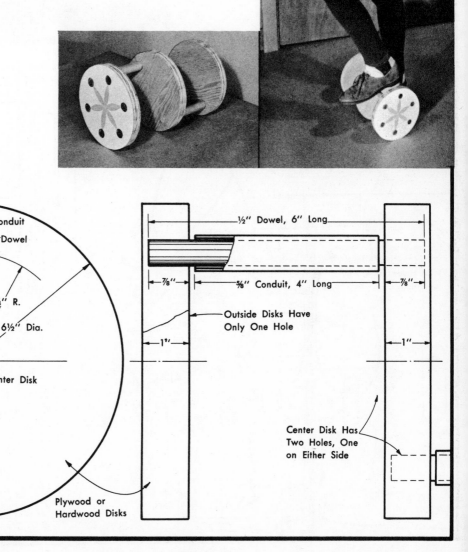

Conduit
Dowel
2¼" R.
6½" Dia.
Center Disk
Plywood or Hardwood Disks

½" Dowel, 6" Long
⅞"
⅝" Conduit, 4" Long
⅞"
Outside Disks Have Only One Hole
1"
1"
Center Disk Has Two Holes, One on Either Side

CLOWN JUMPING JACK

Nail together two pieces of ¼-in. stock to provide the duplicate parts needed for the body, arms, and legs. The head is turned on the lathe — the ⅝-in. projection at the bottom is flattened to ⅜ in. to fit between the body pieces. Use thin brads for all the pivot pins and make the holes for them oversized so that the parts operate freely.

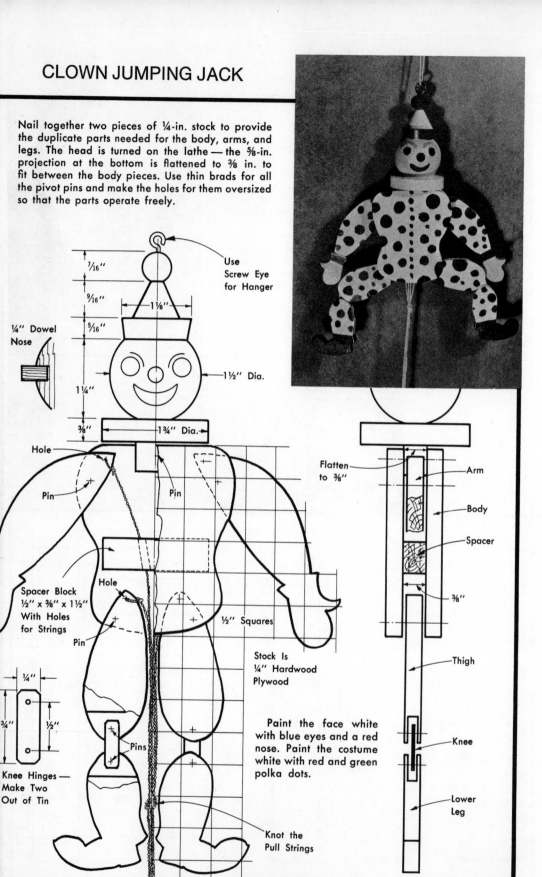

Use Screw Eye for Hanger

⁷⁄₁₆"

⁹⁄₁₆"

1⅛"

⁵⁄₁₆"

¼" Dowel Nose

1½" Dia.

1¼"

⅜"

1¾" Dia.

Hole

Pin

Pin

Flatten to ⅜"

Arm

Body

Spacer

Spacer Block ½" x ⅜" x 1½" With Holes for Strings

Hole

⅜"

Pin

½" Squares

Thigh

¼"

¾"

½"

Pins

Stock Is ¼" Hardwood Plywood

Paint the face white with blue eyes and a red nose. Paint the costume white with red and green polka dots.

Knee

Knee Hinges — Make Two Out of Tin

Knot the Pull Strings

Lower Leg

EASTER BASKETS

It is always nice to have something "different" and these Easter baskets are just that. They are fun to make and fun to play with. The bases are made of plywood. The cutouts can be made of plywood or wallboard or even heavy cardboard. Stack the material for the cutouts, hold together with a brad, and cut several at a time. Glue and nail together the entire assemblies. Paint in light pastel shades of yellow, blue, green, and pink.

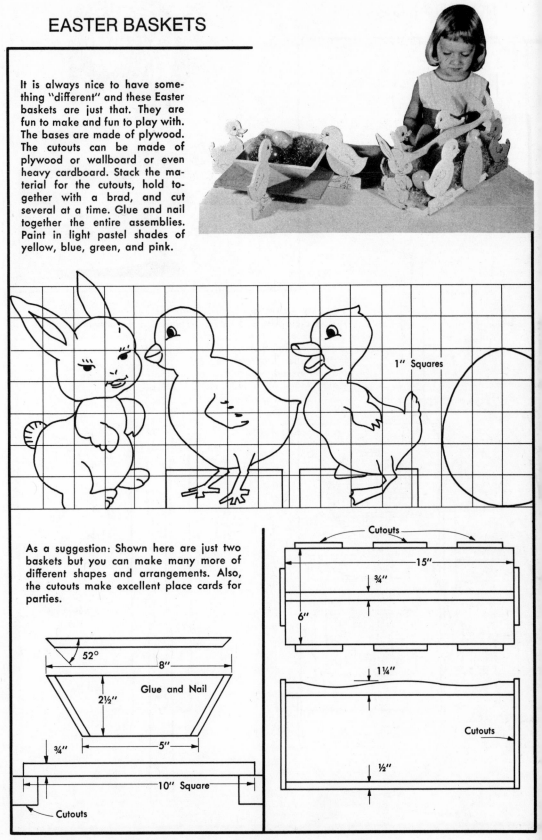

1" Squares

As a suggestion: Shown here are just two baskets but you can make many more of different shapes and arrangements. Also, the cutouts make excellent place cards for parties.

Cutouts

15"

¾"

6"

52°

8"

Glue and Nail

2½"

¾"

5"

10" Square

Cutouts

1¼"

Cutouts

½"

ROGER AND OVER!

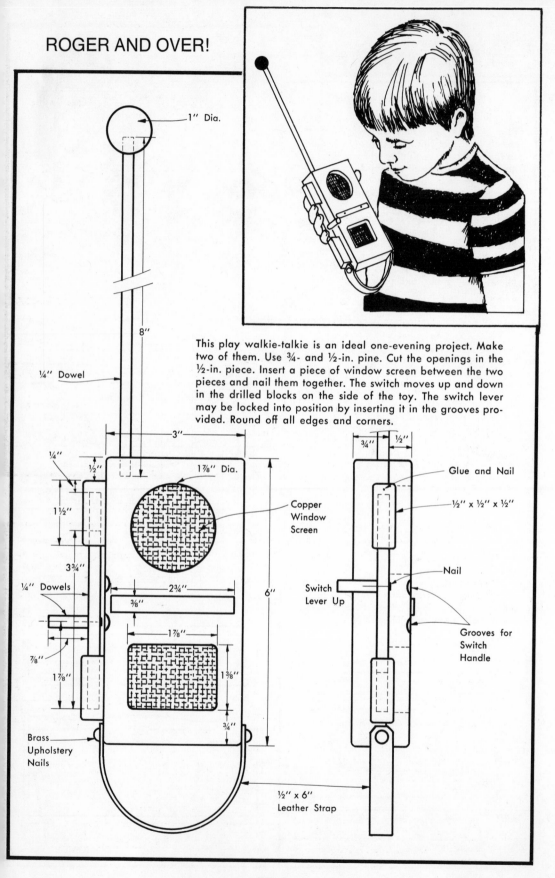

1" Dia.

8"

¼" Dowel

This play walkie-talkie is an ideal one-evening project. Make two of them. Use ¾- and ½-in. pine. Cut the openings in the ½-in. piece. Insert a piece of window screen between the two pieces and nail them together. The switch moves up and down in the drilled blocks on the side of the toy. The switch lever may be locked into position by inserting it in the grooves provided. Round off all edges and corners.

3"

¼"
½"

1½"

1⅞" Dia.

Copper Window Screen

3¾"

¼" Dowels

2¾"

⅜"

1⅞"

6"

⅞"

1⅜"

1⅞"

¾"

Brass Upholstery Nails

½" x 6" Leather Strap

¾"   ½"

Glue and Nail

½" x ½" x ½"

Nail

Switch Lever Up

Grooves for Switch Handle

SIMPLE SANDBOX

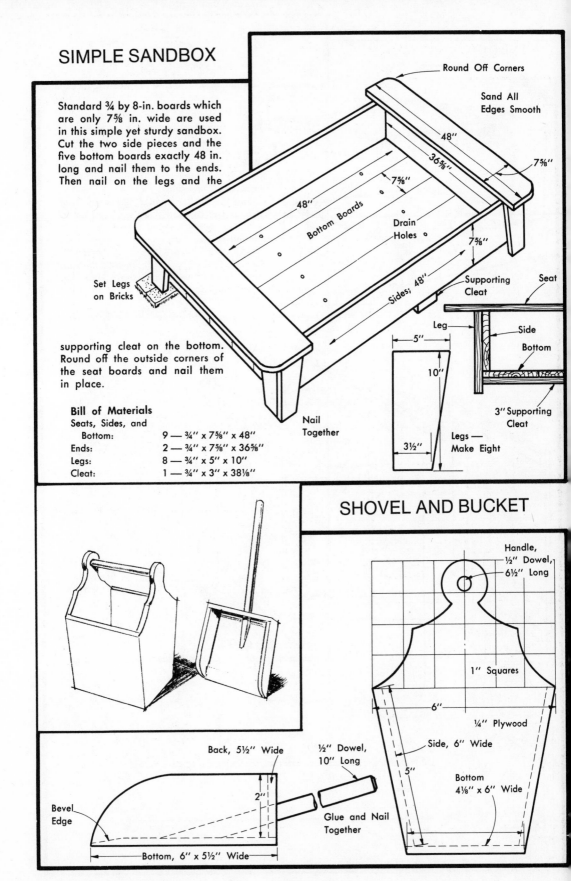

Standard ¾ by 8-in. boards which are only 7⅝ in. wide are used in this simple yet sturdy sandbox. Cut the two side pieces and the five bottom boards exactly 48 in. long and nail them to the ends. Then nail on the legs and the

Round Off Corners

Sand All Edges Smooth

48"

36⅝"

7⅝"

48"

Bottom Boards

7⅝"

Drain Holes

7⅝"

Sides, 48"

Set Legs on Bricks

Supporting Cleat

Seat

Leg

Side

Bottom

5"

10"

3½"

3" Supporting Cleat

Legs — Make Eight

supporting cleat on the bottom. Round off the outside corners of the seat boards and nail them in place.

Nail Together

Bill of Materials

Seats, Sides, and
Bottom: 9 — ¾" x 7⅝" x 48"
Ends: 2 — ¾" x 7⅝" x 36⅝"
Legs: 8 — ¾" x 5" x 10"
Cleat: 1 — ¾" x 3" x 38⅛"

SHOVEL AND BUCKET

Handle,
½" Dowel,
6½" Long

1" Squares

6"

¼" Plywood

Side, 6" Wide

5"

Bottom
4⅛" x 6" Wide

Back, 5½" Wide

½" Dowel,
10" Long

Glue and Nail Together

Bevel Edge

2"

Bottom, 6" x 5½" Wide

FANCY SANDBOX

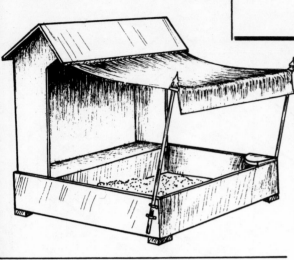

Here is a sandbox that is practical and at the same time attractive. It is made entirely of ¾ x 10 in. (9⅝ in.) white-pine boards. The legs are pieces of 2 x 4, 4 in. long. Make the box first. The bottom is nailed to the 1½ in. strips that extend around the bottom of the sides. Next fit in the uprights, the back, and roof pieces. The roof should be covered with roofing paper. Then make the toy storage box with the hinged cover. If an awning is desired, as shown, make it 4 x 4 ft. and support it with the cross brace and ¾-in. dowels that are held in place with pipe straps. Turn the ornamental finials on the lathe. Paint the entire box.

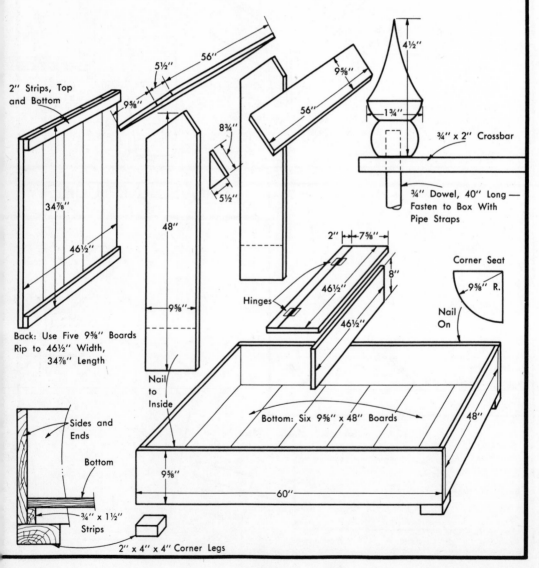

2" Strips, Top and Bottom

5½"
56"
9⅝"
9⅝"
56"

8¾"

5½"

4½"

1¾"

¾" x 2" Crossbar

¾" Dowel, 40" Long — Fasten to Box With Pipe Straps

34⅞"

46½"

48"

9⅝"

Back: Use Five 9⅝" Boards Rip to 46½" Width, 34⅞" Length

Nail to Inside

Hinges

2"   7⅝"
46½"
8"
46½"

Corner Seat

9⅝" R.

Nail On

Bottom: Six 9⅝" x 48" Boards

48"

Sides and Ends

Bottom

9⅝"

60"

¾" x 1½" Strips

2" x 4" x 4" Corner Legs

72

TOTE CART

This can serve as both a toy and a handy cart useful for many chores. It is simple to build, with the use of standard materials. The box is made of ½-in. plywood. The axle is a 2 by 4 and the wheels are made of 1⅝ by 9⅝-in. plank. Nail the box together and then screw on the handle, axle, and front support. The wheels run on ⅜ by 6-in. lag screws threaded into the axle. Be sure to drill the axle accurately for these lag screws so that the wheels run true. When completed, give the entire cart several coats of high-quality outdoor paint.

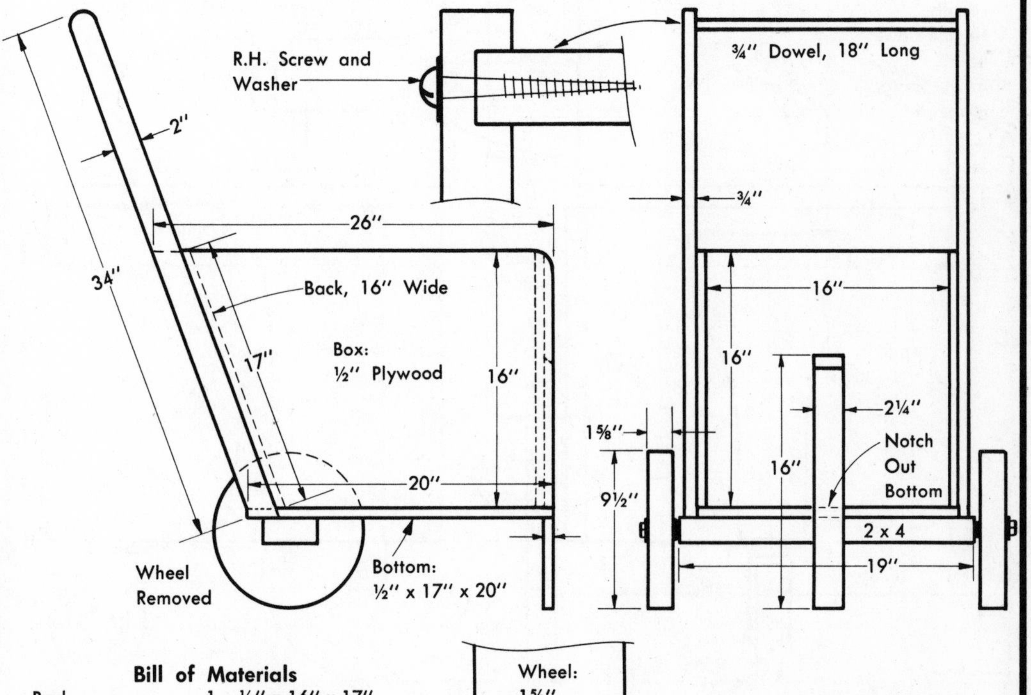

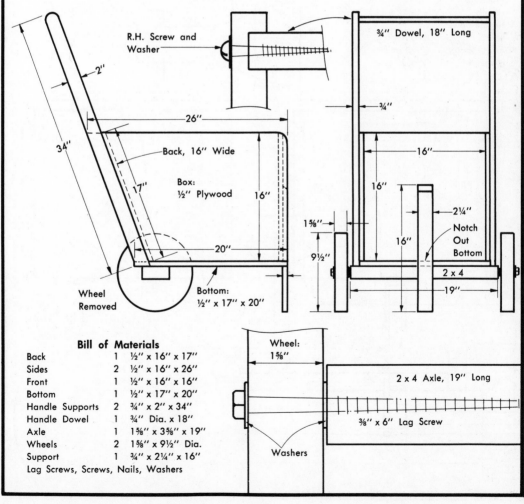

R.H. Screw and Washer
¾'' Dowel, 18'' Long
2''
¾''
26''
34''
Back, 16'' Wide
17''
Box:
½'' Plywood
16''
16''
16''
2¼''
1⅝''
Notch Out Bottom
16''
9½''
20''
2 x 4
19''
Wheel Removed
Bottom:
½'' x 17'' x 20''

Bill of Materials

Back	1	½'' x 16'' x 17''
Sides	2	½'' x 16'' x 26''
Front	1	½'' x 16'' x 16''
Bottom	1	½'' x 17'' x 20''
Handle Supports	2	¾'' x 2'' x 34''
Handle Dowel	1	¾'' Dia. x 18''
Axle	1	1⅝'' x 3⅝'' x 19''
Wheels	2	1⅝'' x 9½'' Dia.
Support	1	¾'' x 2¼'' x 16''

Lag Screws, Screws, Nails, Washers

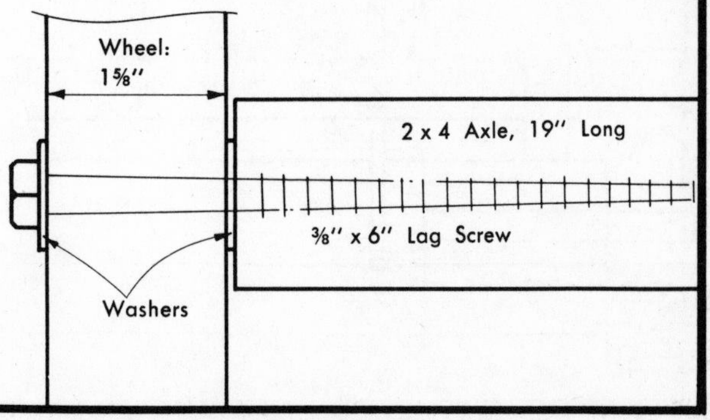

Wheel:
1⅝''
2 x 4 Axle, 19'' Long
⅜'' x 6'' Lag Screw
Washers

TOY STORAGE CART

This project is excellent for training youngsters to be neat and tidy. Cut the pieces accurately and perfectly square and nail and glue together. Make the axle block with the two ¾-in. axle dowels and attach wheels using dowel pins or cotter keys. Bolt the axle block to the cart and screw the 5-in. swivel caster in place. Hinge the handle to the front and then cut and hinge the top in place. The entire unit may be painted inside and out and decorated with decals.

Bill of Materials

Bottom	¾" x 16" x 26½" Plywood
Sides 2	¾" x 14" x 28" Plywood
Ends 2	¾" x 14" x 16" Plywood
Top 1	¾" x 18½" x 29" Plywood
Axle Block	1⅝" x 2¼" x 18½"
Axles 2	¾" Dowel x 5"
Wheels 2	1⅛" x 9¼" Dia.
Handle	¾" x 7" x 13"
Handle Dowel	½" x 7"
Bolts 2	⅜" x 3½"
Swivel Caster	5" Wheel
Hinges 4	¾" x 2"

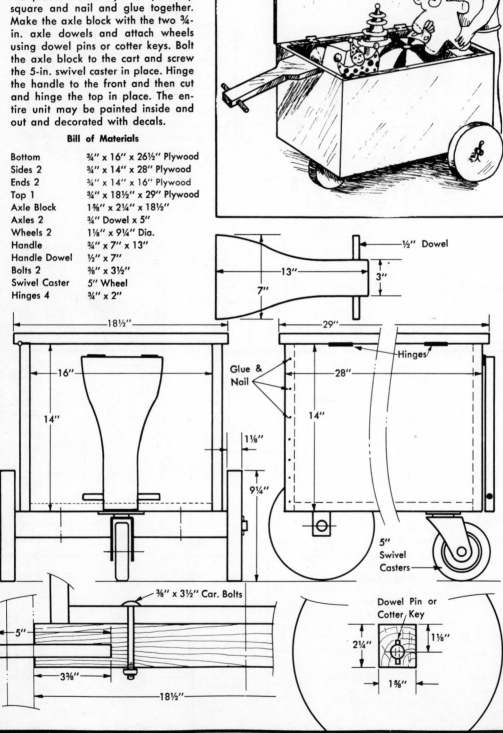

½" Dowel

13"

7"

3"

18½"

29"

16"

Glue & Nail

Hinges

28"

14"

14"

1⅛"

9¼"

5" Swivel Casters

⅜" x 3½" Car. Bolts

Dowel Pin or Cotter Key

5"

3⅜"

18½"

2¼"

1⅛"

1⅝"

ALL-WOOD KIDDIE CAR

This sturdy Kiddie Car is quite simple to build, and if it is made out of hardwood, it will last for years and years. The most exacting work is the construction of the steering handle. It consists of two parts; the upper part, which is 1¾ in. square, is turned on the lathe to a 1¼-in. diameter. It has a 2½ in. section at the lower end turned to a 1-in. diameter which fits through the seat and into the 1-in. hole in the lower part of the handle. The lower part of the handle is also 1¾ in. square and has a ⅞-in. slot for the front wheel. The upper and lower parts of the handle are held together by a ¼ x 2-in. carriage bolt.

The axles are ¾-in. dowels. The wheels, ¾ in. thick and 5 in. in diameter, are held to the axles by means of ¼-in. dowel pins. Screw the entire unit together as shown and give it several coats of high-gloss enamel.

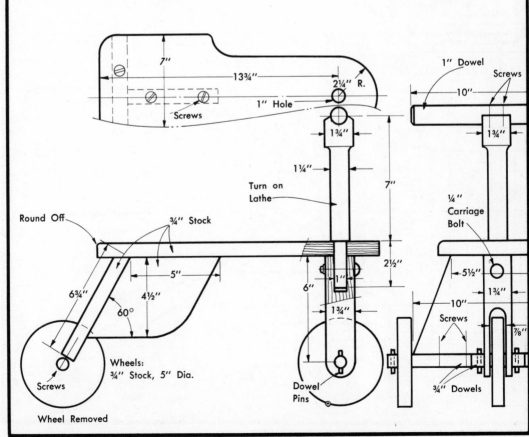

HEAVY KIDDIE CAR

This entire toy is made of 1⅛-in. stock which does add to its weight but at the same time allows it to withstand rough handling. It is quite simple to make. The handle uprights, handle, front axle, and main frame are 1⅛ x 1⅛-in. stock. The rear axle is a 1-in. dowel. Three-inch casters are used for the front wheels. Be sure to check the height of the casters and adjust the length of the handle uprights **A** so that the seat remains horizontal. The unit is bolted and screwed together for strength. If made of hardwood the toy may be given a coat of clear lacquer or it may be enameled in white with bright trim.

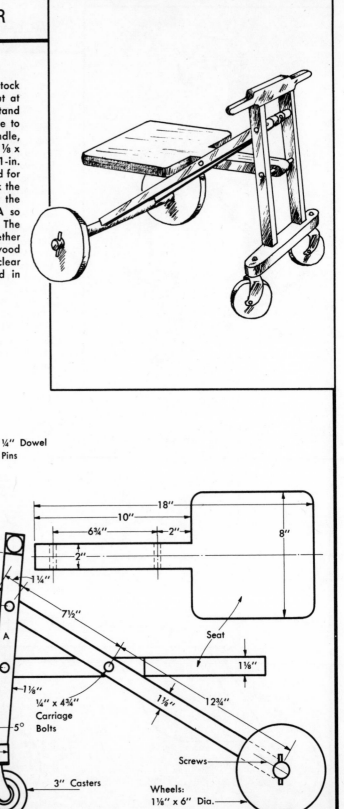

1⅛"
1⅛"
2"
Screws
¼" Dowel Pins
13½"
1" Dowel
1⅛"
12½"
2¾"
1⅛"
1"
Screws
¼" x 2¾" Carriage Bolts
3¼"
1¼"
7½"
1⅛"
3⅞"
A
¼" x 7" Carriage Bolt
4¾"
1⅛"
¼" x 4¾" Carriage Bolts
5°
14"
2"
Screws
1⅛"
3" Casters
18"
10"
6¾"
2"
2"
8"
Seat
1⅛"
1⅛"
12¾"
Screws
Wheels: 1⅛" x 6" Dia.

ROCKING HORSE 1

Follow this procedure to avoid errors and waste of material: Just cut the four legs and the two rockers first. Then cut the brace-spacers (A) and (B), two of each. Assemble the legs to the rockers and screw the brace-spacers in place. This provides the base for the entire unit. Next cut the side pieces, being certain that the tops are even where the seat will rest. Screw these in place against the legs. The most difficult part of this job is fitting parts (C) and (D), the bases for the neck and tail. Compound angles must be made and the only way to make them is to cut and fit. Screw (C) and (D) in place. Then make the neck and head and the tail, remove (C) and (D), and screw the neck from below onto (C) and the

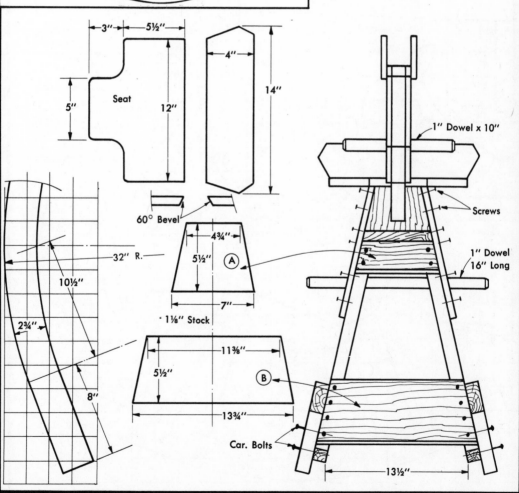

Seat

3″ 5½″

5″ 12″ 14″

4″

60° Bevel

32″ R.

10½″

2¾″

8″

4¾″

5½″ (A)

7″

1⅛″ Stock

11⅜″

5½″ (B)

13¾″

Car. Bolts

1″ Dowel x 10″

Screws

1″ Dowel 16″ Long

13½″

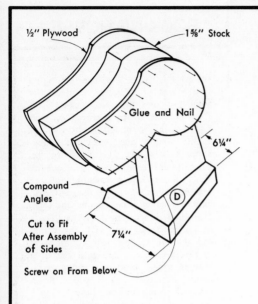

½″ Plywood

1⅝″ Stock

Glue and Nail

6¼″

Compound Angles

Cut to Fit After Assembly of Sides

7¼″

D

Screw on From Below

tail onto (D). Finally, make the seat and drill the hole through the neck for the hand rest and through the sides for the footrests. Enamel the entire unit to suit.

Bill of Materials

Sides, Head, and Ears	½″ Plywood, 24″ x 28″
Head, Neck, and Tail	1⅝″ x 12″ x 12″
Legs (4)	1⅛″ x 3½″ x 24″
C Base for Tail	1⅛″ x 2½″ x 5″
A Top Leg Brace (2)	¾″ x 5½″ x 7¼″
B Bottom Leg Brace (2)	¾″ x 5½″ x 13¾″
Rockers (2)	1⅛″ x 7⅝″ x 40″
D Base for Neck	1⅛″ x 7″ x 6¼″
Seat	¾″ x 8½″ x 12″
Seat Back	¾″ x 4″ x 14″
Handle	1″ Dowel x 10″
Footrest	1″ Dowel x 16″

Four, ⅜″ x 2¾″ Carriage Bolts
1″, 1¼″ and 3″ Screws

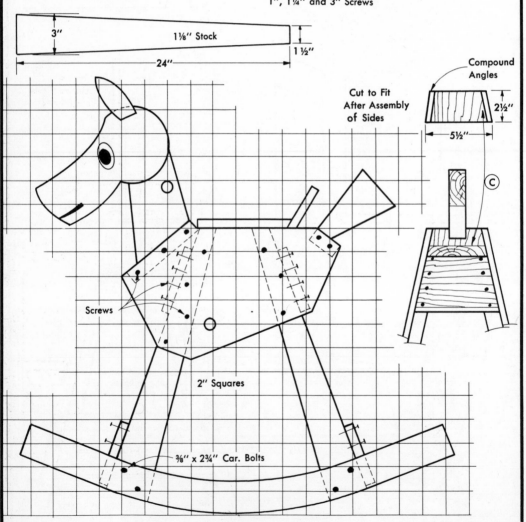

3″

1⅛″ Stock

1½″

24″

Compound Angles

Cut to Fit After Assembly of Sides

2½″

5½″

C

Screws

2″ Squares

⅜″ x 2¾″ Car. Bolts

ROCKING HORSE 2

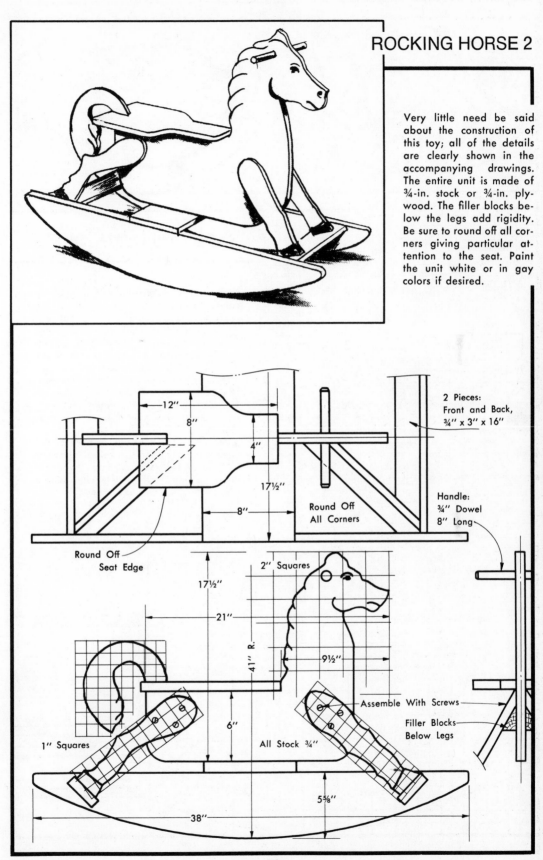

Very little need be said about the construction of this toy; all of the details are clearly shown in the accompanying drawings. The entire unit is made of ¾-in. stock or ¾-in. plywood. The filler blocks below the legs add rigidity. Be sure to round off all corners giving particular attention to the seat. Paint the unit white or in gay colors if desired.

2 Pieces:
Front and Back,
¾" x 3" x 16"

12"

8"

4"

17½"

Round Off
All Corners

Handle:
¾" Dowel
8" Long

8"

Round Off
Seat Edge

17½"

21"

2" Squares

41" R.

9½"

6"

1" Squares

Assemble With Screws

Filler Blocks
Below Legs

All Stock ¾"

5⅝"

38"

SAFE CHILD'S ROCKERS

Here are two rockers that afford complete safety for the child. The curves of the rockers at the bottom are very flat and long, the seats are conveniently low, and the sides are wide apart so there is little danger of tipping in any direction. Make the sides of ¾-in. plywood and be sure all corners are well rounded and sanded. The backrests, seats, and the footrest on the duck design may be made of ¾-in. white pine or plywood if desired. To provide added rigidity, "glue blocks" may be glued under the seat and in back of the backrests. The handle on each rocker is a 1-in. dowel mortised into the sides. Paint the entire unit in white with suitable trim in blue, yellow, and orange.

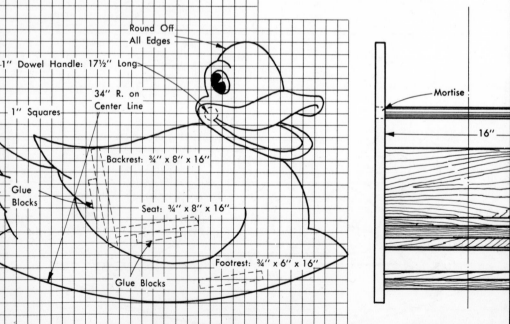

1" Dowel Handle: 17½" Long

Glue Blocks

22½" R. on Center Line

Seat: ¾" x 8" x 16"

1" Squares

Backrest: ¾" x 11" x 16"

Round Off All Edges

1" Dowel Handle: 17½" Long

34" R. on Center Line

1" Squares

Backrest: ¾" x 8" x 16"

Glue Blocks

Seat: ¾" x 8" x 16"

Footrest: ¾" x 6" x 16"

Glue Blocks

Mortise

16"

ANOTHER ROCKER

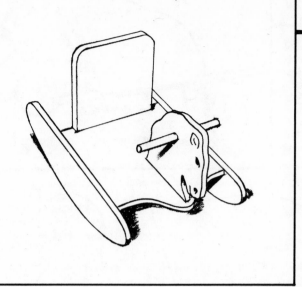

There is no danger that a tot will fall out of this rocker because it is designed to be low and not easily tipped. The entire unit may be made of ¾-in. white pine or ¾-in. plywood or a combination of both if you have the materials on hand. Glue and screw the parts together and be sure to round off and sand all edges and corners. When completed give the rocker an undercoat and finish with white or light-colored enamel.

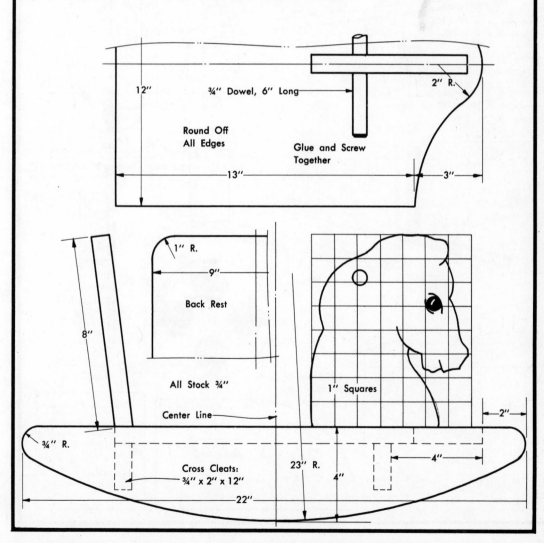

12"

¾" Dowel, 6" Long

2" R.

Round Off
All Edges

Glue and Screw
Together

13"

3"

1" R.

9"

Back Rest

8"

All Stock ¾"

1" Squares

2"

Center Line

¾" R.

23" R.

4"

4"

Cross Cleats:
¾" x 2" x 12"

22"

81

UTILITY WHEELBARROW

The construction of this child's wheelbarrow presents no unusual problems. The duck is made of 1-in. stock with ⅜-in. plywood sides. The 1-in. block extends only as far as indicated by the dotted line to provide a cavity for the 5-in. diameter wheel. Paint the wheel as shown to represent feet for the duck. A metal bushing will prolong the life of the wheel. Paint the duck yellow and the remaining parts white.

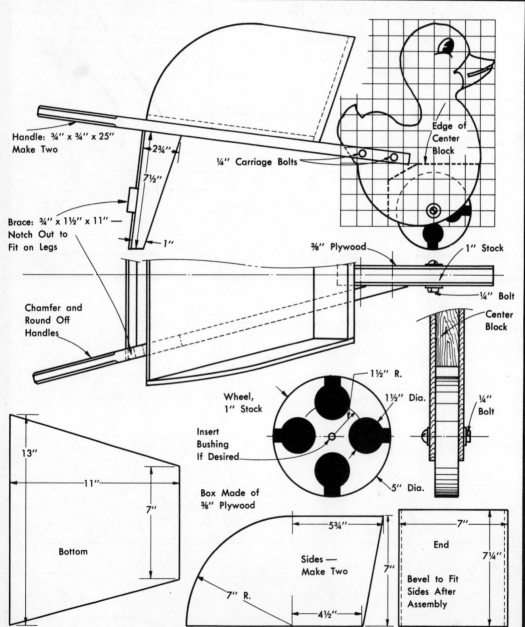

Handle: ¾" x ¾" x 25"
Make Two

2¾"

7½"

¼" Carriage Bolts

Brace: ¾" x 1½" x 11" —
Notch Out to
Fit on Legs

1"

Edge of
Center
Block

⅜" Plywood

1" Stock

¼" Bolt

Center
Block

Chamfer and
Round Off
Handles

Wheel,
1" Stock

1½" R.

1½" Dia.

¼"
Bolt

Insert
Bushing
If Desired

5" Dia.

Box Made of
⅜" Plywood

13"

11"

7"

Bottom

Sides —
Make Two

5¾"

7"

7" R.

4½"

End

Bevel to Fit
Sides After
Assembly

7"

7¼"

82

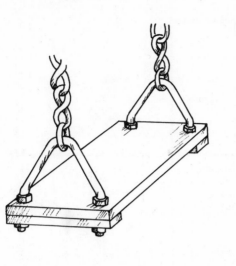

Because of the U-bolts which support the swing, it is impossible to tip the seat, thus making this swing exceptionally safe. Make a form out of 1⅛-in. stock as shown below, right, for forming the two ⅜-in. rod U-bolts. After forming them, thread the ends as indicated. Then make the seat out of oak and drill the ⅜-in. holes to take the U-bolts. Use ⅜-in. chain for supporting the swing. Fasten the chain to the limb as shown, using a ⅜-in. bolt and washers and a piece of split garden hose between the chain and limb to protect the tree.

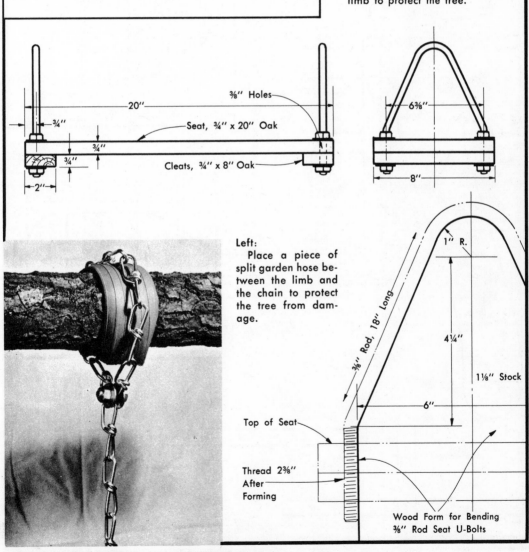

20″

⅜″ Holes

¾″

¾″

¾″

2″

Seat, ¾″ x 20″ Oak

Cleats, ¾″ x 8″ Oak

6⅜″

8″

Left:
Place a piece of split garden hose between the limb and the chain to protect the tree from damage.

1″ R.

⅜″ Rod, 18″ Long

4¼″

1⅛″ Stock

6″

Top of Seat

Thread 2⅜″ After Forming

Wood Form for Bending ⅜″ Rod Seat U-Bolts

INDOOR SWING

This sturdy swing affords something different in the way of indoor play for children. It is suspended by means of three ⅜-in. ropes, two at the front of the swing that support the handle bar and the stirrup bar and one at the back that supports the seat. This arrangement provides flexibility yet makes the swing perfectly safe, since there is no danger of tipping. This is an ideal swing for basement use where the ropes may be attached to an overhead joist. It is made of 1⅛-in. white pine and hardwood dowels.

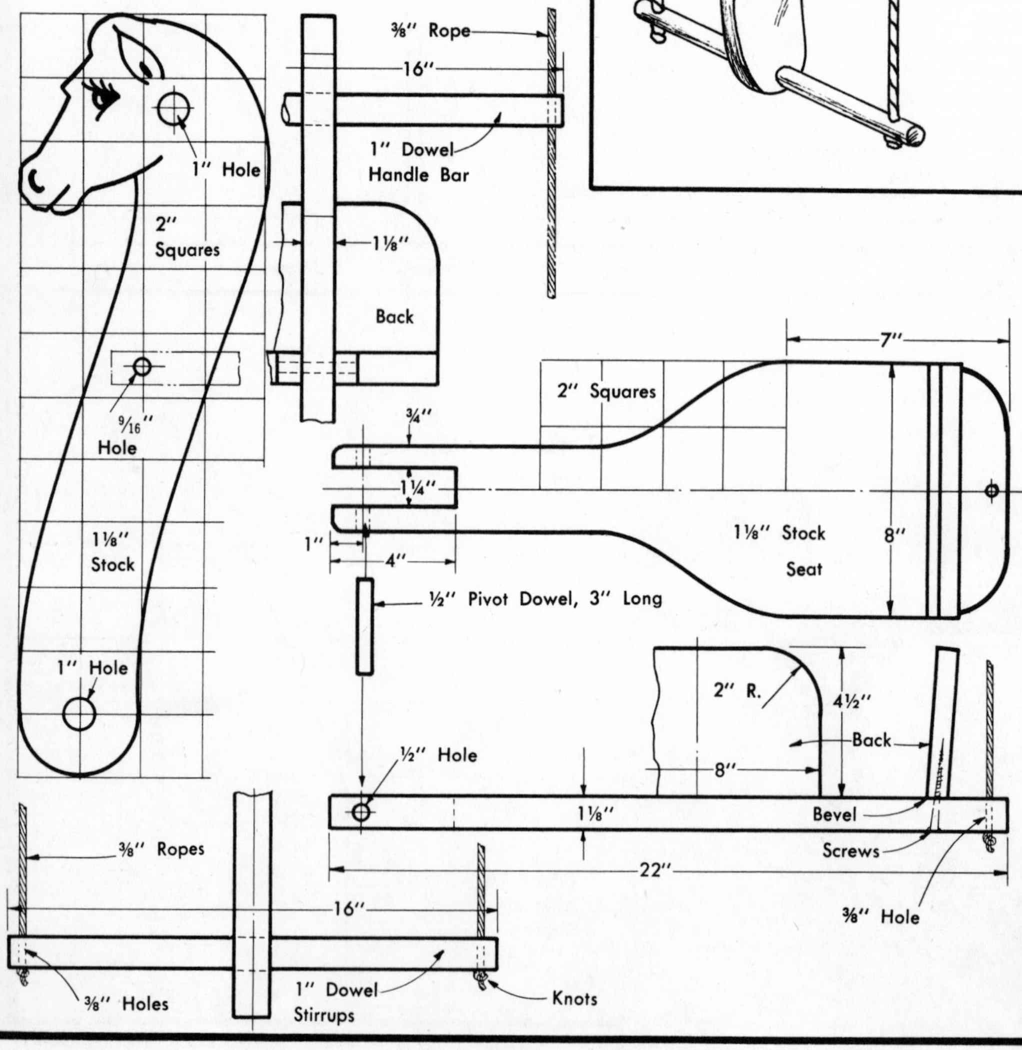

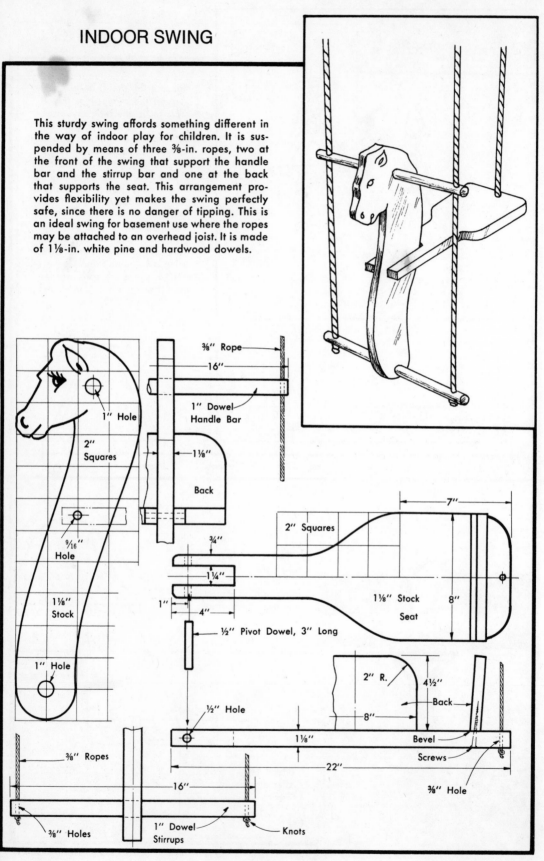

1" Hole
2" Squares
9/16" Hole
1⅛" Stock
1" Hole
⅜" Rope
16"
1" Dowel Handle Bar
1⅛"
Back
7"
2" Squares
¾"
1¼"
1"
4"
1⅛" Stock
Seat
8"
½" Pivot Dowel, 3" Long
2" R.
4½"
Back
8"
½" Hole
1⅛"
Bevel
Screws
22"
⅜" Hole
⅜" Ropes
16"
⅜" Holes
1" Dowel
Stirrups
Knots

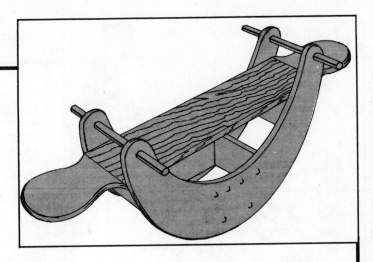

This is a safe, practical toy that will provide hours of fun as well as healthful exercise. It may be used indoors and out.

Make four curved segments as indicated out of ¾-in. plywood and form the two rocker sides by bolting two of the pieces together using ⅜ x 2-in. carriage bolts. Then cut spacers A and B and assemble by screwing the pieces together. Next, cut the seat out of 1⅛-in. stock and secure it in place with wood screws. Cut the 1-in. dowel handles and insert them in the holes in the side pieces.

Enamel the finished Teeter-Totter in bright colors: red and green; red and yellow; orange and blue.

Bill of Materials

Side Pieces	4	Plywood	¾" x 12½" x 28"
Cleats	2		¾" x 8" x 14"
Spacers (A)	2		1⅛" x 8" x 12"
Spacers (B)	2		¾" x 8" x 13½"
Seat	1		1⅛" x 9½" x 84"
Handles	2		1" Dowel x 20"

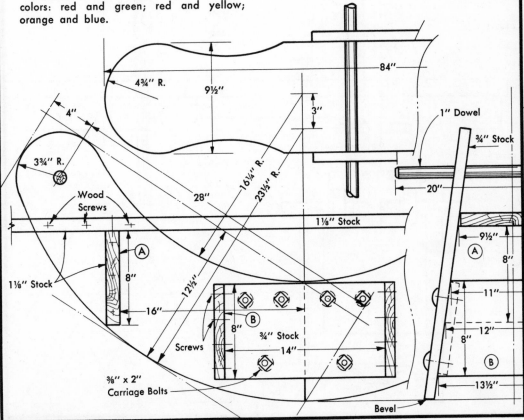

TEETER-TOTTER 2

This teeter-totter has two chief features. There is a bumper beneath each seat to prevent the hands or feet from being pinched. Also the main plank may be moved into different positions on the balance point to compensate for differences in weight. The construction is quite simple. To hold the 1-in. pipe in place, a pipe strap may be added to both sides as shown. Use heavy, long screws in assembling the unit.

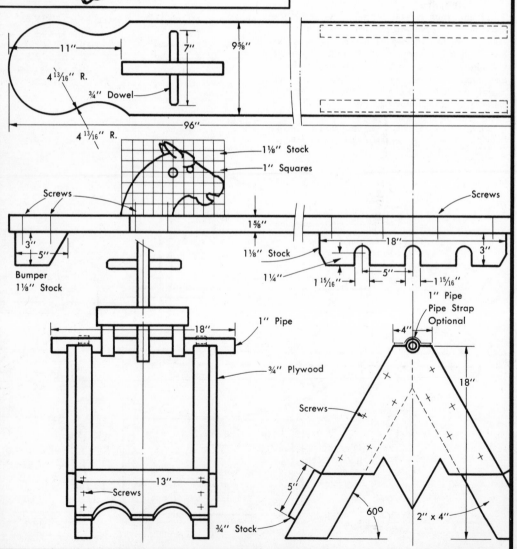

11″

$4^{13}/_{16}$″ R.

¾″ Dowel

7″

$9^{5}/_{8}$″

$4^{13}/_{16}$″ R.

96″

1⅛″ Stock

1″ Squares

Screws

Screws

1⅝″

Bumper
1⅛″ Stock

3″

5″

1⅛″ Stock

1¼″

18″

3″

$1^{15}/_{16}$″

5″

$1^{15}/_{16}$″

1″ Pipe
Pipe Strap
Optional

4″

18″

18″

1″ Pipe

¾″ Plywood

Screws

13″

Screws

¾″ Stock

5″

60°

2″ x 4″

PLAYHOUSE

The 2 by 2-in. frames for the sides, back, and front may be made indoors and then assembled on the wooden or concrete base out-of-doors. All stock is of standard sizes so that a minimum of cutting and fitting is necessary. Use outdoor, waterproof ¼-in. plywood for the exterior. Cover the roof ridge with a sheet-metal cap 6 in. wide to make the roof rainproof. The window frames and screens may be eliminated if desired. Paint the playhouse to match the other buildings on the property.

Bill of Materials

Frame	24 — 2'' x 2'' x 12'0''
Trim and Braces	10 — ¾'' x 3⅝'' x 10'0''
Fascia	2 — ¾'' x 1⅝'' x 6'0''
Windows	2 — ¾'' x 1½'' x 12'0''
Sheeting	1 — ¼'' x 4' x 4' exterior plywood
	1 — ¼'' x 4' x 10' exterior plywood
	4 — ¼'' x 4' x 8' exterior plywood
Base	3 — 2'' x 4'' x 8'0''
Floor	7 — ¾'' x 6'' x 8'0''

Nails, Hinges, Screening, Molding, Cedar Posts

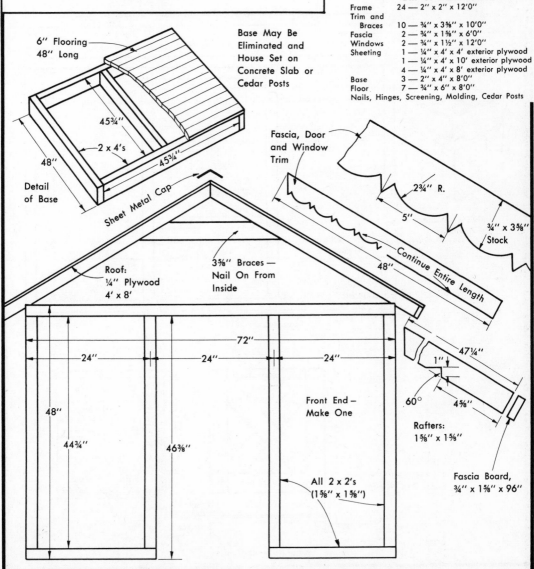

6'' Flooring 48'' Long

Base May Be Eliminated and House Set on Concrete Slab or Cedar Posts

45¾''

2 x 4's

48''

45¾''

Detail of Base

Sheet Metal Cap

Fascia, Door and Window Trim

2¾'' R.

5''

¾'' x 3⅝'' Stock

Continue Entire Length

48''

Roof: ¼'' Plywood 4' x 8'

3⅝'' Braces — Nail On From Inside

72''

24''   24''   24''

48''

44¾''

46⅜''

Front End — Make One

All 2 x 2's (1⅝'' x 1⅝'')

47¼''

1''

60°

4⅝''

Rafters: 1⅝'' x 1⅝''

Fascia Board, ¾'' x 1⅝'' x 96''

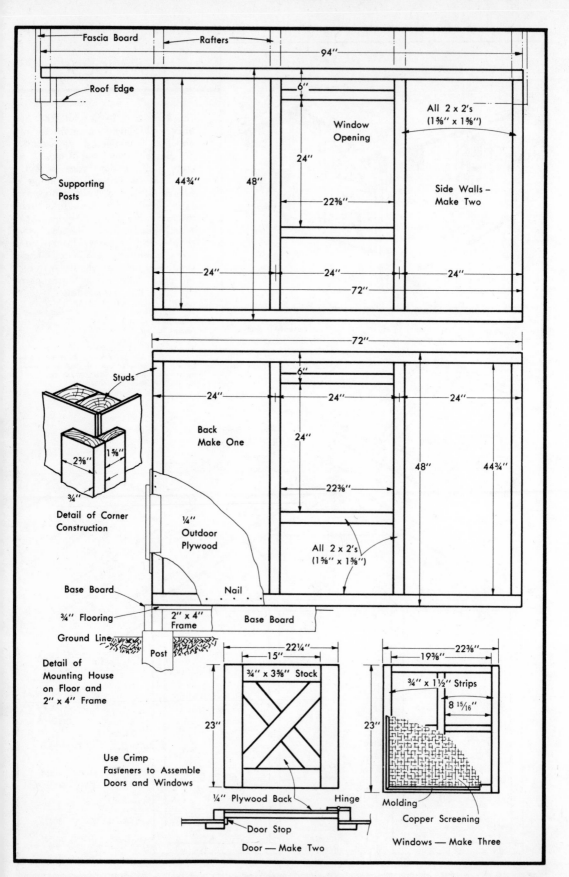

Fascia Board — Rafters — 94"

Roof Edge

Supporting Posts

6"

Window Opening

24"

All 2 x 2's (1⅝" x 1⅝")

Side Walls – Make Two

44¾"   48"   22⅜"

24"   24"   24"

72"

Studs

Detail of Corner Construction

2⅜"   1⅝"

¾"

72"

6"

24"   24"   24"

Back Make One

24"   48"   44¾"

22⅜"

¼" Outdoor Plywood

All 2 x 2's (1⅝" x 1⅝")

Base Board

¾" Flooring   2" x 4" Frame   Base Board

Nail

Ground Line

Post

Detail of Mounting House on Floor and 2" x 4" Frame

22¼"
15"

¾" x 3⅝" Stock

23"

22⅜"
19⅜"

¾" x 1½" Strips

8 15/16"

23"

Use Crimp Fasteners to Assemble Doors and Windows

¼" Plywood Back   Hinge

Door Stop

Door — Make Two

Molding

Copper Screening

Windows — Make Three

LITTLE CROOKED HOUSE

Here is a children's favorite, the Little Crooked House of storybook fame — a playhouse that will thrill any youngster on Christmas morning or any other morning. It will be a welcome addition to any backyard and large enough to accommodate several children plus their toys. The Crooked House is designed to be built in panels and painted **indoors** and then bolted together **outdoors**. This is a fine project for winter evenings. The design was created by a leading building materials manufacturer and special permission was granted to show the plans here. Most of the larger lumber dealers are familiar with these plans, so if you have any questions they will be happy to help you and also supply any materials needed. For an attractive finish, use chocolate brown with white trim on the outside, a light gray-green on the inside, and sand color on the floor. Don't worry about making a few mistakes in construction. It's a Crooked House, so who will recognize them?

Bill of Materials

2 — ¾" x 4' x 6' exterior plywood	Roof rafters, floor
1 — ¾" x 2' x 6' exterior plywood	Roof rafters
2 — ¼" x 4' x 8' exterior plywood	Front, back walls
2 — ¼" x 4' x 6' exterior plywood	Side walls
5 — 2" x 4" x 12' stock lumber	Plates, framing
12 — 2" x 4" x 8' stock lumber	Ridge, framing, sills
1 — 1" x 4" x 8' stock lumber	Rafter ties
2 — 1" x 4" x 10' stock lumber	Trim
2 — 1" x 6" x 8' stock lumber	Flower boxes
20 — 1" x 2" x 8' stock lumber	Battens
80 sq. ft. — 1" x 6" sheathing	Roof sheathing
1 square (100 sq. ft.)	USG thick butt shingles
50' roll	15# asphalt felt
6 — 8" x 8" x 16" cement blocks	Foundation
Paint, nails, as needed	

NOTE: Although the materials' list is for an 8-ft. playhouse, you can increase the size by enlarging the squared patterns to 9-in. squares instead of 6-in. as indicated. Refigure the materials you will need accordingly.

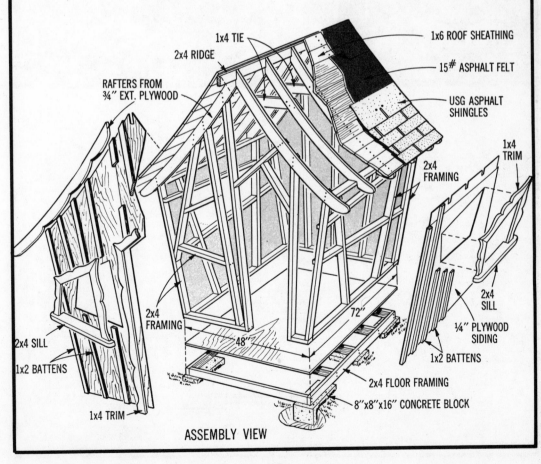

1x4 TIE
2x4 RIDGE
RAFTERS FROM ¾" EXT. PLYWOOD
1x6 ROOF SHEATHING
15# ASPHALT FELT
USG ASPHALT SHINGLES
2x4 FRAMING
1x4 TRIM
2x4 FRAMING
2x4 SILL
1x2 BATTENS
1x4 TRIM
2x4 SILL
¼" PLYWOOD SIDING
1x2 BATTENS
2x4 FLOOR FRAMING
8"x8"x16" CONCRETE BLOCK
48"
72"

ASSEMBLY VIEW

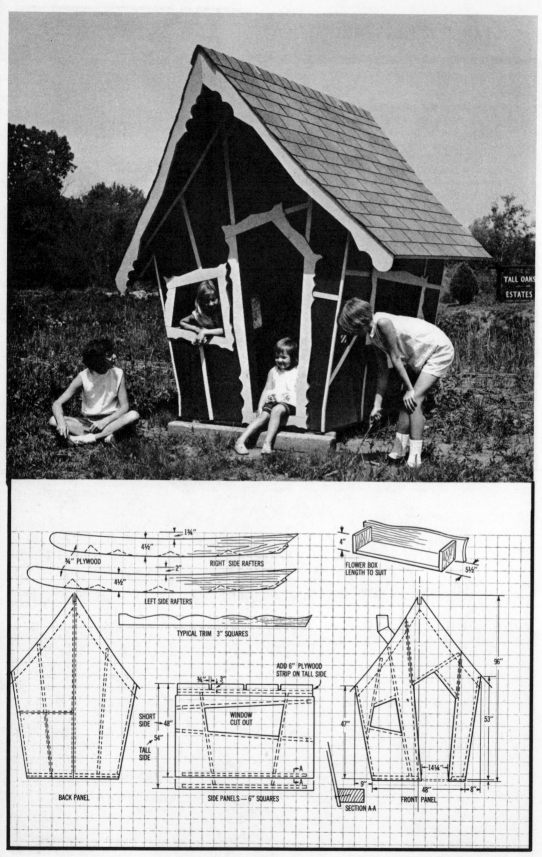

¾" PLYWOOD

1¾"

4½"

RIGHT SIDE RAFTERS

2"

4"

FLOWER BOX
LENGTH TO SUIT

5½"

4½"

LEFT SIDE RAFTERS

TYPICAL TRIM 3" SQUARES

ADD 6" PLYWOOD
STRIP ON TALL SIDE

¾" 3"

WINDOW
CUT OUT

SHORT
SIDE 48"

54"

TALL
SIDE

96"

53"

47"

14¼"

9"

48"

8"

BACK PANEL

SIDE PANELS — 6" SQUARES

A

A

SECTION A-A

FRONT PANEL

90

SCALE LUMBER

At first glance, these pictures seem to show the construction of a real building. Actual construction is shown but instead of full-size lumber, scale lumber has been used. Construction with scale lumber permits the young carpenter to learn firsthand how buildings are put up and at a minimum of expense, yet basic operations performed in full-scale construction can be exactly duplicated but in miniature.

A scale of 3 in. to 1 ft. is generally considered practical. This is one fourth actual size. With this scale the individual pieces of wood are not too small to be nailed as in full-scale work, yet they are large enough to be easily handled, cut, and nailed. The best wood to use is basswood since it has virtually no grain and is easily cut and nailed without danger of splitting. Cut the basswood on the circular saw using a hollow ground blade so that no further sanding or finishing is required.

For information on building construction, most libraries carry a number of excellent books on carpentry. These books will provide the building details for which you will be looking. Further it may be noted that this is an ideal method for use in vocational and adult education schools.

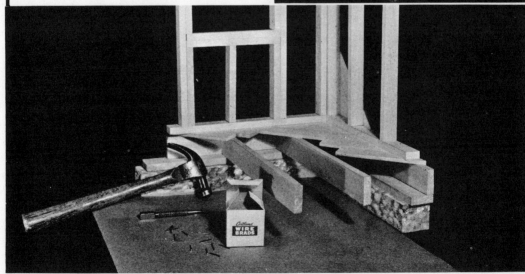

This special clock face is used to teach children how to tell time. The hour hand points to the large dots next to the hour figures; the minute hand extends well beyond the hour figures and points to the minutes located outside of the face. The hands are held onto the face by means of a wing nut and bolt so that either hand may be removed for concentration on the other hour or minute hand and figures. Each hand is plainly marked. The unit shown here was made of heavy white cardboard. The figures were cut out of a calendar. Note the words "After" and "To" on the minute dial.

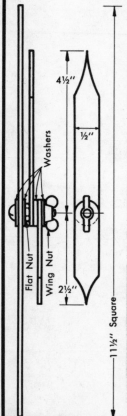

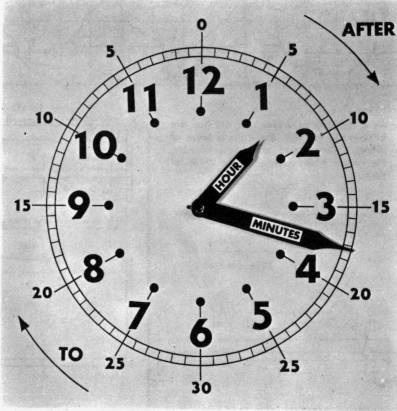

JOINTED HORSE

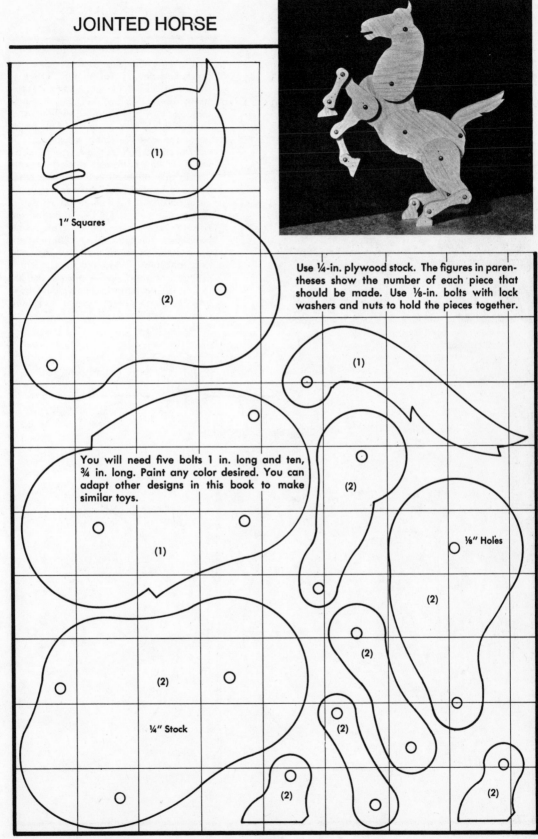

1" Squares

(1)

(2)

(1)

Use ¼-in. plywood stock. The figures in parentheses show the number of each piece that should be made. Use ⅛-in. bolts with lock washers and nuts to hold the pieces together.

(2)

(1)

⅛" Holes

You will need five bolts 1 in. long and ten, ¾ in. long. Paint any color desired. You can adapt other designs in this book to make similar toys.

(2)

(2)

(2)

(2)

(2)

¼" Stock

(2)

(2)

This is a new version of the ancient toy, "spin-the-button." To spin a button (it should be about 1½ in. in diameter), a string about 48 in. long is threaded through two opposite holes and then knotted into a loop as shown. If the button is rotated and the string wound upon itself, a slight pull outward on the string will twirl the button at a high speed—first in one direction and then the other. Cut a 5-in.-diameter disk out of white cardboard and color it on both sides as shown. Cement to it a 1½-in. button and twirl as explained above. Watch what happens to the colors: they disappear and other colors take their places. The outer ring becomes gray, the next ring is orange, the third ring is purple, and the center is green. Incidentally, this shows how the three primary colors, red, blue, and yellow, are mixed to make other colors.

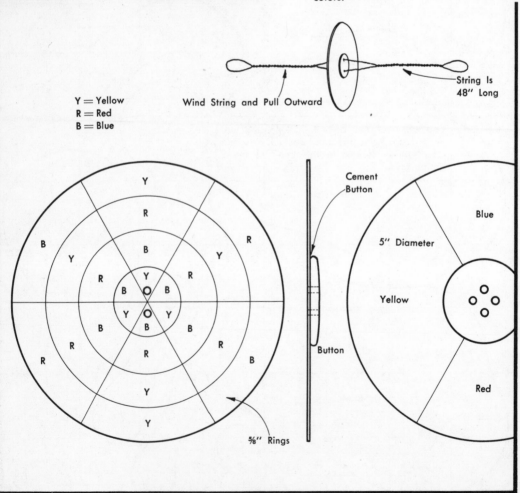

Y = Yellow
R = Red
B = Blue

Wind String and Pull Outward

String Is 48" Long

Cement Button

5" Diameter

Blue

Yellow

Red

Button

⅝" Rings

CUP AND BALL GAME

This is a one-evening project easily made out of maple or other hardwood. The cup may be finished with clear lacquer and the ball in bright red or green. A rubber ball may be substituted for the wood ball. A fine hole is drilled in the wooden ball, counterbored at one end for the knot of the string. The 30-in. string is tied to the cup handle. This project makes a fine game of skill.

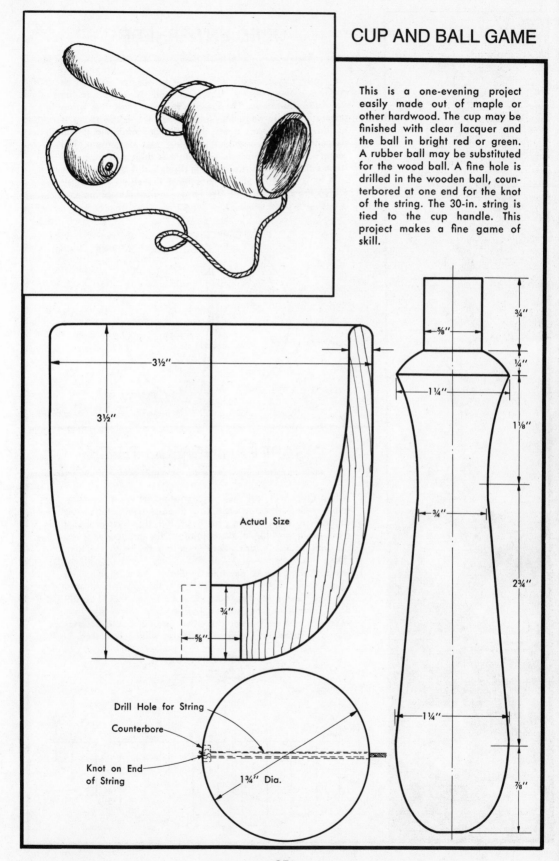

3½"

3½"

Actual Size

¾"

⅝"

¾"

⅝"

1¼"

¾"

¼"

1⅛"

2¾"

1¼"

⅞"

Drill Hole for String

Counterbore

Knot on End of String

1¾" Dia.

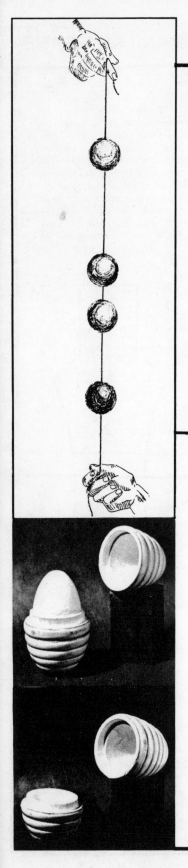

OBEDIENT SPHERE

This little bit of magic will puzzle grown-ups as well as children. The wooden sphere or ball does just as the magician demands. To operate it, show that the string passes freely through the sphere, yet, when the string is pulled taut the sphere will not fall! On command it will descend to any point on the string and stay there. The secret? The hole through the sphere is drilled at an angle from either end. As the string is tightened it binds and the sphere is held in place. Loosening the string just a bit allows the sphere to fall. Use hardwood for the sphere and a heavy twisted cord, 22 in. long.

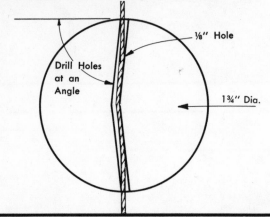

Drill Holes at an Angle

⅛" Hole

1¾" Dia.

DISAPPEARING-EGG TRICK

This project will test the craftsmanship of even the most experienced woodturner. It is a three-part unit that nests together to form the egg as illustrated. It is best made of close-grain maple. In manipulation, the magician opens the unit at the upper joint, revealing the egg. He then closes it, places the end with the hole to his lips, and pretends that he sucks out and swallows the egg. He then again opens the unit, but this time at the lower joint, and the egg seemingly has disappeared. When this is deftly done, it will not be noticed that a different section has been opened each time. However, no one should be permitted to handle the egg or the secret will be revealed.

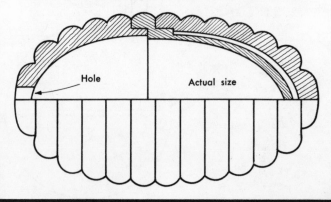

Hole

Actual size

NOW YOU SEE IT... NOW YOU DON'T!

The disappearing coin trick is an old one, but it is just as mystifying today as is was years ago. The secret is in the double compartment, and when the box is deftly handled by the magician, the coin will vanish and reappear at command. Of course, you can't allow the audience to examine the box because the secret would be revealed. This toy is a challenge to the lathe operator. It is best turned out of hard maple, with the sections fitting snugly so they will stay together. The dimensions may vary from those shown but be certain that the bead sections are exactly the same width so the joints will not be detected. Give the box several coats of clear lacquer or varnish.

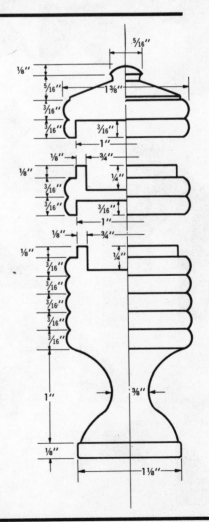

CHINESE TANGRAM

This is a mysterious Chinese toy, perhaps thousands of years old, yet as modern as tomorrow. Use thin material such as cardboard or ⅛-in. fiberboard and divide a square into seven pieces as indicated below. By arranging these pieces into various combinations a countless number of figures and designs may be obtained. Just a few of them are shown. Tangram designs are ideal for creating abstract, eye-catching figures for school posters, displays, and illustrations. Working with tangrams challenges the imagination and provides hours of creative fun. Contests featuring Chinese tangram designs will attract interest in both school and home.

DOUBLE SQUARE

Here you have 14 pieces with which to work in a great variety of shapes to form a large number of figures and designs.

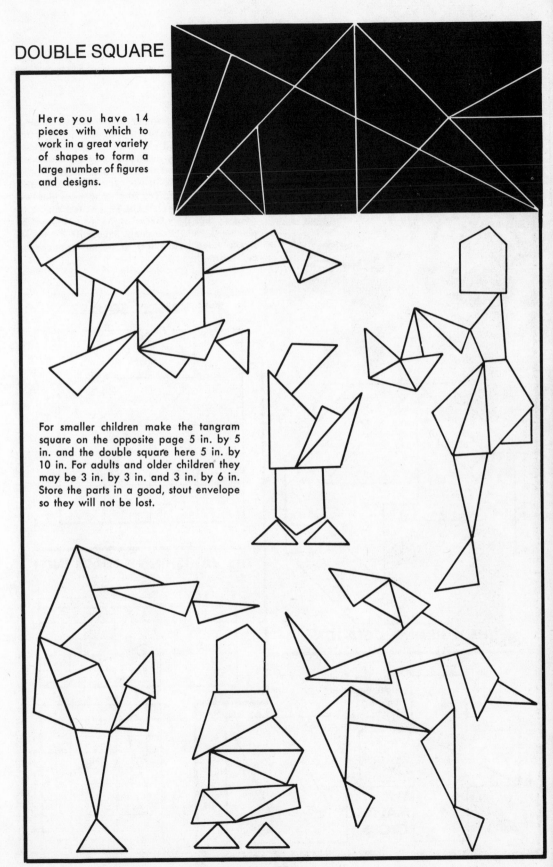

For smaller children make the tangram square on the opposite page 5 in. by 5 in. and the double square here 5 in. by 10 in. For adults and older children they may be 3 in. by 3 in. and 3 in. by 6 in. Store the parts in a good, stout envelope so they will not be lost.

PIECE PUZZLES

Here are four popular and intriguing piece puzzles. They will challenge the analytical ability of both young and old. Although the pieces may be made of heavy cardboard, they are best made of ½-in. fiberboard that is smooth on both sides. Make the cuts with the finest fret saw available for maximum accuracy and sand the edges and corners. Both sides should be painted the same color so that the identity of the parts will not be revealed. The "Vanishing Square Inch" puzzle should have inch marks drawn or scribed on it as indicated.

THE YANKEE SQUARE

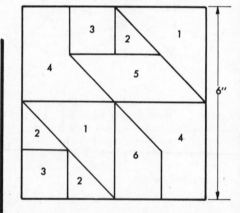

THE WHIRLING OCTAGON

THE VANISHING SQUARE INCH

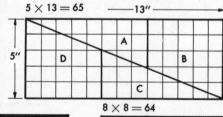

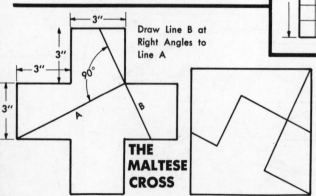

THE MALTESE CROSS

Draw Line B at Right Angles to Line A

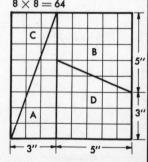

SOLITAIRE PEG CHECKERS

This game is played by jumping a peg over an adjoining peg into a vacant hole. The "jumped" peg is removed. The purpose of the game is to clear the board with only one peg remaining. If you want to make it more difficult, have that last peg land in the center hole. The game usually starts with the center hole vacant. This is a good lathe project. However, if you do not have a lathe, make the board in the shape of a Maltese cross or an octagon. The pegs are ¼-in. dowel formed by clamping the dowel in the lathe or drill-press chuck. Make 32 pegs and a few extra to replace those that will become lost. Any suitable wood may be used.

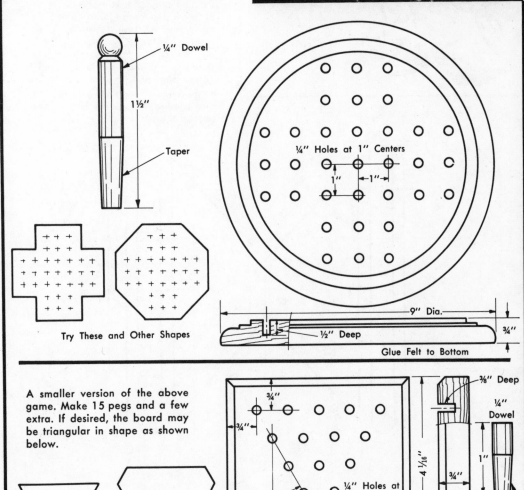

¼" Dowel

1½"

Taper

¼" Holes at 1" Centers

1"   1"

Try These and Other Shapes

9" Dia.

½" Deep

¾"

Glue Felt to Bottom

A smaller version of the above game. Make 15 pegs and a few extra. If desired, the board may be triangular in shape as shown below.

¾"

¾"

30°

¼" Holes at ¾" Centers

4 1/16"

¾"

4½"

¾"

⅜" Deep

¼" Dowel

¾"

1"

Taper

Bevel

DIABOLO

This fascinating toy probably originated in China a long time ago. It was very popular in France and England in the eighteenth and nineteenth centuries. It requires just as much skill to operate it today as it did then. To start the spool spinning, it is rolled along the floor by manipulating the two sticks with the string. When it is spinning rapidly, the object is to toss the spool in the air and catch it on the string. This sounds simple but it takes a great deal of practice. The Diabolo is a type of "yo-yo."

The Diabolo is an ideal one-evening project. It is made of maple or other hardwood, and turned on the lathe. Be sure to make it accurately so that it balances perfectly on the string and therefore runs smoothly. The sticks are ⅝-in. dowels, 18 in. long, and tapered to 5/16 in. at the ends. The string is ⅛-in. soft cord knotted through the holes in the ends of the sticks.

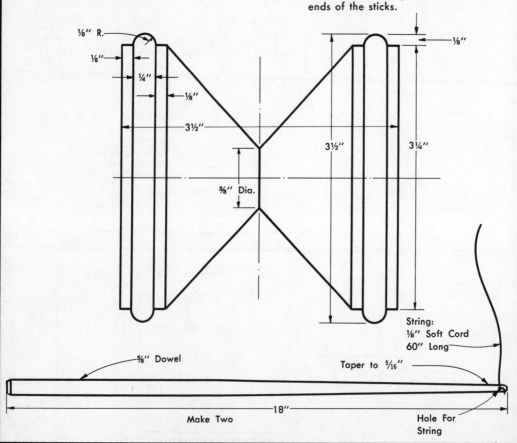

⅛" R.

⅛"

¼"

⅛"

3½"

⅝" Dia.

⅛"

3½"

3¼"

String:
⅛" Soft Cord
60" Long

⅝" Dowel

Taper to 5/16"

Make Two

18"

Hole For String

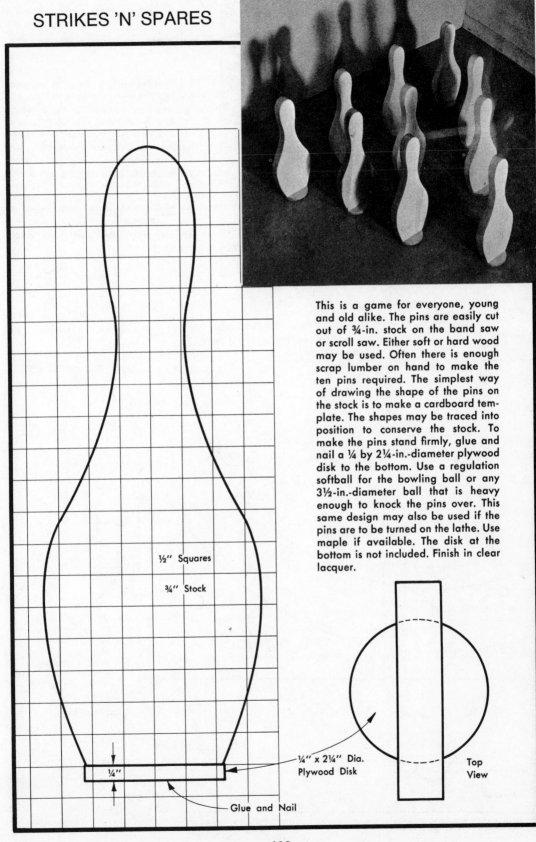

½" Squares

¾" Stock

This is a game for everyone, young and old alike. The pins are easily cut out of ¾-in. stock on the band saw or scroll saw. Either soft or hard wood may be used. Often there is enough scrap lumber on hand to make the ten pins required. The simplest way of drawing the shape of the pins on the stock is to make a cardboard template. The shapes may be traced into position to conserve the stock. To make the pins stand firmly, glue and nail a ¼ by 2¼-in.-diameter plywood disk to the bottom. Use a regulation softball for the bowling ball or any 3½-in.-diameter ball that is heavy enough to knock the pins over. This same design may also be used if the pins are to be turned on the lathe. Use maple if available. The disk at the bottom is not included. Finish in clear lacquer.

¼"

¼" x 2¼" Dia. Plywood Disk

Top View

Glue and Nail

SPIN-A-BEAD

This is a fascinating game for old and young. The object is to spin the top and see how many of the eight beads fall into the pockets. The top is turned out of hardwood, and the two round-headed nails propel the beads. The 5/16-in. diameter beads come from a variety store. In turning the bowl be certain that the inside wall is undercut as shown; if not, the force of the top will shoot the beads out of the bowl. This is a fine one-evening project. Finish the bowl with clear lacquer.

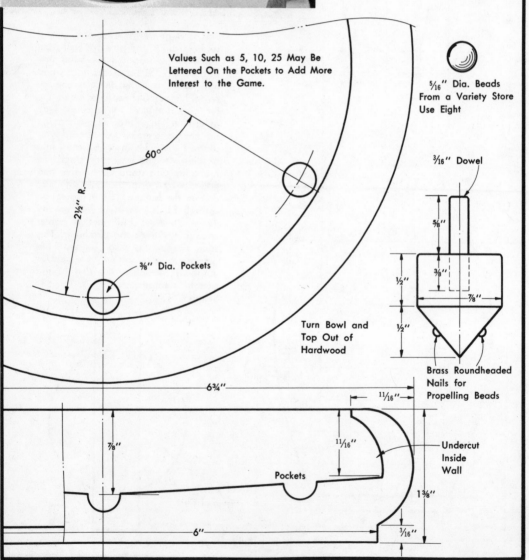

Values Such as 5, 10, 25 May Be Lettered On the Pockets to Add More Interest to the Game.

60°

2½" R.

⅜" Dia. Pockets

Turn Bowl and Top Out of Hardwood

5/16" Dia. Beads From a Variety Store Use Eight

3/16" Dowel

5/8"

3/8"

½"

7/8"

½"

Brass Roundheaded Nails for Propelling Beads

6¾"

11/16"

7/8"

Pockets

11/16"

Undercut Inside Wall

1⅜"

6"

3/16"

Part 2
HOW TO
MAKE WHEELS

Wheels are important in the construction of toys. A wheel that wobbles or runs "out of true" often makes a toy inoperable, and detracts from appearance of the toy and the fun of playing with it. On the other hand, true-running, well-balanced wheels add much to the quality and enjoyment of the toy.

Making true-running wheels is not as difficult as it may seem, since there are many ways to produce them. The following methods are the most practical and simple ways of making wheels.

Hand-Cut Wheels

The simplest way to make a wheel is to scribe a circle of the required diameter on the stock, using either a pencil compass or a divider. When the circle is scribed, the wheel may be cut by hand, using an ordinary coping saw as shown in Figure 1. The hole at the center should be carefully drilled and the raw sawed edge of the wheel should be sanded smooth. If care is taken when sawing and in locating the axle hole, a fairly accurate wheel can be made. Do not discard your scraps or odd pieces of stock — they may be converted into wheels.

Machine-Cut Wheels

If you possess a band saw or a scroll saw, the cutting of accurate wheels is greatly simplified. Here again, the outline of the wheel should be scribed on the stock and then cut on the band or scroll saw as illustrated in Figure 2. The pivot or axle hole is drilled as mentioned above and the edges should be sanded smooth.

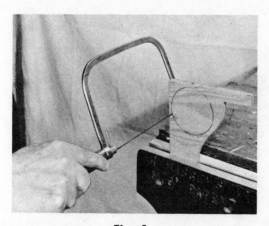

Fig. 1

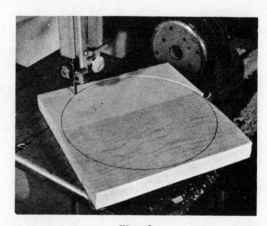

Fig. 2

Fig. 3

Machine-Cut Wheels Made with a Jig

The use of a centering jig on either the band saw or the scroll saw will enable you to make superior wheels. They will be perfectly round, of uniform size and diameter, and they will run true on the preselected centers.

Figures 3 and 4 show a jig of this type and Figure 5 shows how it is built. A ½-in. plywood table is clamped to the saw table. It has a ½ x ½-in. slot which holds a ½ x ½-in. sliding wood bar. This bar has a sharp center point. The bar is moved toward or away from the saw blade to the correct radius for the wheels to be made and it is then clamped into position by means of the thumbscrew below the table.

In operation, the center of the stock is marked and the center is then punch-marked with a fine nail. This punch mark is then placed over the center point on the sliding bar and thus held in place. As the stock is revolved around the point, the saw blade cuts the stock, making an accurate circle. **Precaution:** Be certain that the center point on the bar is at a precise right angle with the path of the blade. If not, the cut will lead into or away from the true path, and the wheel will not be perfectly round.

Another Saw Jig

Another jig is shown in Figures 6 and 7, and Figure 8 shows how it is made. Again a ½-in. plywood table is clamped to the table of the band saw or scroll saw. This plywood table has a series of ⅛-in. holes drilled on

Fig. 4

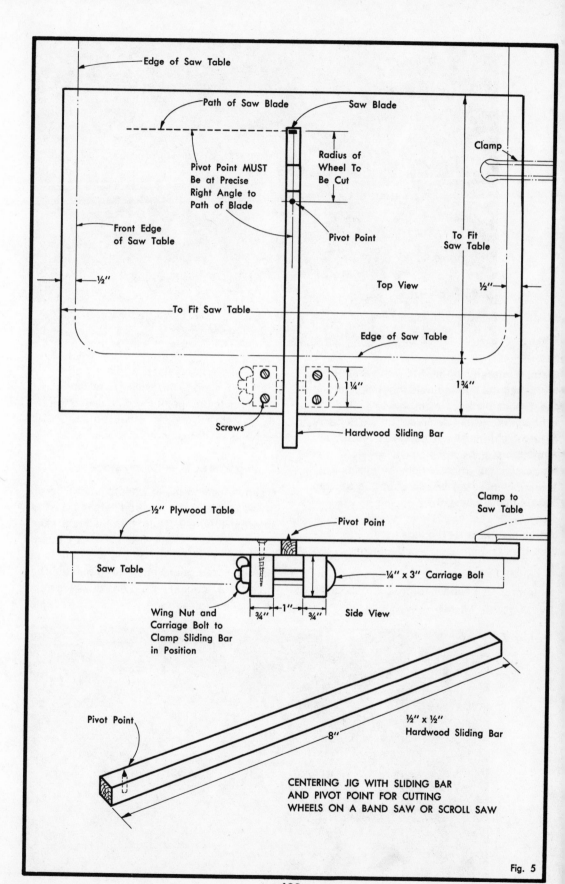

Edge of Saw Table

Path of Saw Blade

Saw Blade

Clamp

Pivot Point MUST Be at Precise Right Angle to Path of Blade

Radius of Wheel To Be Cut

Front Edge of Saw Table

Pivot Point

To Fit Saw Table

½"

Top View

½"

To Fit Saw Table

Edge of Saw Table

1¼"

1¾"

Screws

Hardwood Sliding Bar

½" Plywood Table

Pivot Point

Clamp to Saw Table

Saw Table

¼" x 3" Carriage Bolt

Wing Nut and Carriage Bolt to Clamp Sliding Bar in Position

¾" 1" ¾"

Side View

Pivot Point

8"

½" x ½" Hardwood Sliding Bar

CENTERING JIG WITH SLIDING BAR AND PIVOT POINT FOR CUTTING WHEELS ON A BAND SAW OR SCROLL SAW

Fig. 5

Fig. 6

½-in. centers along a straight line. A ⅛-in. metal peg fits into the hole that is located at the proper distance from the saw blade to produce the wheel desired. The stock has a ⅛-in. hole drilled in the center and is slipped over the peg. As the stock is revolved, the blade cuts the wheel. Again, be certain that the location of the hole and peg is at right angles to the saw path.

Additional Uses for the Jigs

The wheel-cutting jigs shown here and on the preceding page may also be used on the table of a disk sander to produce accurate, true-running wheels. The stock may be rough-cut by hand and then placed on the jig that is clamped to the table of the sander. As the stock is brought into contact with the revolving abrasive disk, it will be shaped to size and sanded smooth at the same time.

Cutting Wheels from Round Stock

A simple way to make wheels is to slice off round stock in the desired thicknesses as shown in Figure 9. (**Note:** For this picture the saw is not in operation and the saw guard has been removed. When the machine is in operation, **the guard must be in place.**) The material being cut is 1½-in. dowel stock, also called "closet pole," which is available

Fig. 7

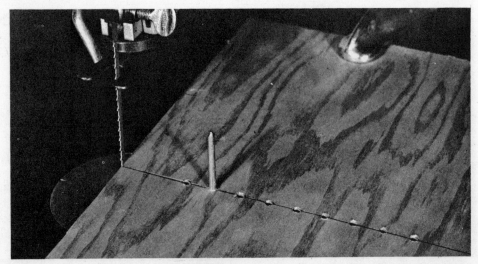

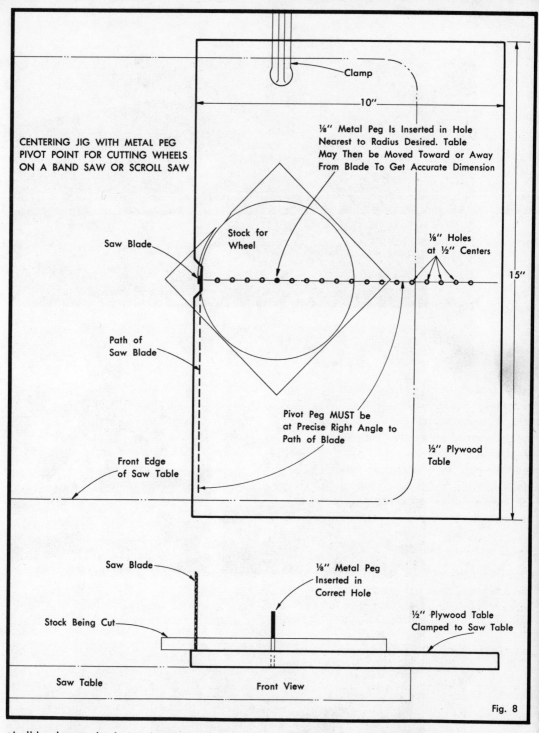

CENTERING JIG WITH METAL PEG
PIVOT POINT FOR CUTTING WHEELS
ON A BAND SAW OR SCROLL SAW

Clamp

10"

15"

⅛" Metal Peg Is Inserted in Hole
Nearest to Radius Desired. Table
May Then be Moved Toward or Away
From Blade To Get Accurate Dimension

Saw Blade

Stock for
Wheel

⅛" Holes
at ½" Centers

Path of
Saw Blade

Pivot Peg MUST be
at Precise Right Angle to
Path of Blade

½" Plywood
Table

Front Edge
of Saw Table

Saw Blade

⅛" Metal Peg
Inserted in
Correct Hole

Stock Being Cut

½" Plywood Table
Clamped to Saw Table

Saw Table

Front View

Fig. 8

at all lumberyards. A stop has been clamped to the saw table so that uniform pieces ⁵⁄₁₆-in. thick may be cut.

The problem with wheels made in this way is to locate the center after they are cut. This is simply done by means of a center square clamped onto the bar of the combination square. Use the tool as shown in Figure 10 and mark the stock. Then turn the tool at

right angles and mark the stock again. The point at which the two marks intersect is the center of the wheel and the axle hole should be drilled here.

Round stock may be cut on the circular saw, as illustrated, or on the band saw or by means of a hand-operated miter saw as shown in Figure 11. If you do not have a

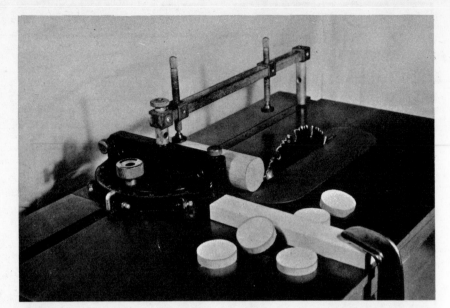

Fig. 9

Fig. 10

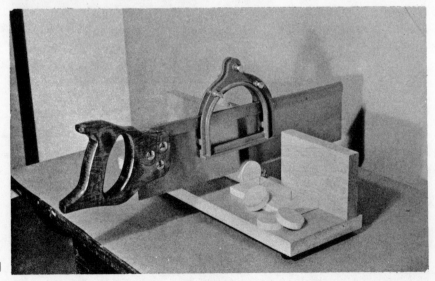

Fig. 11

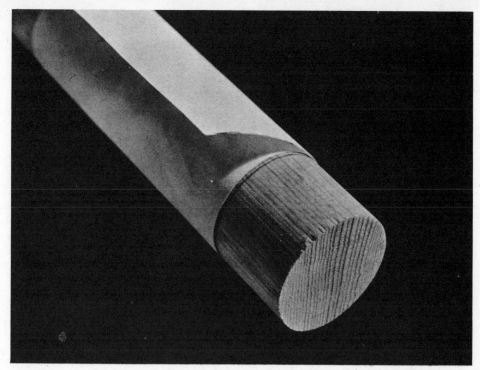

Fig. 12

Fig. 13

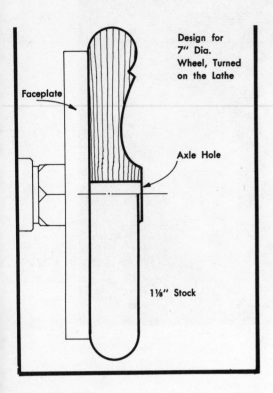

Design for
7" Dia.
Wheel, Turned
on the Lathe

Faceplate

Axle Hole

1⅛" Stock

miter saw to make the cut square with the axis of the round stock, you can provide a guideline for the saw cut by first wrapping a piece of straight-edged heavy paper around the stock as shown in Figure 12. Then use the edge of the paper to mark the stock, and when you saw along this line, the cut will be square with the axis of the stock.

Making Wheels on the Lathe

The lathe is the most versatile power tool for the production of accurately made wheels. The most common procedure is to cut the stock to its approximately finished diameter and then mount it on the faceplate. This is an excellent method for making large wheels. As shown in Figure 13, the stock may be turned to resemble a tire and hub or other design. The axle hole is drilled or turned also.

For smaller wheels the stock should be end-squared and mounted on a small faceplate. A hole of the diameter of the wheel mounting

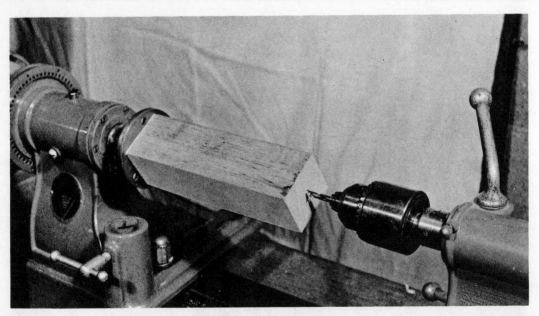

Fig. 14

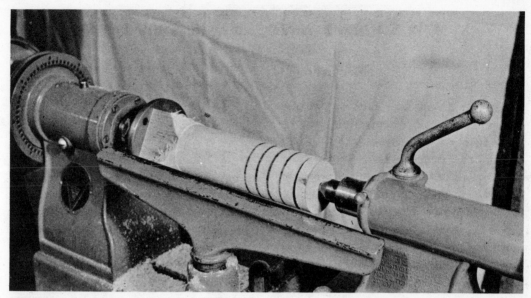

Fig. 15

screw should be drilled at dead center about 1½-in. deep as illustrated in Figure 14. A 60-degree bevel dead-end center should be used in the actual turning as illustrated in Figure 15.

The stock is now turned to the desired diameter and a wheel is cut off at the dead end. The stock is then drilled again, the bevel center is used, and another wheel is cut off. This operation is repeated until the desired number of wheels is made. The advantage of this method is that all the wheels will be of the same diameter and the axle holes will be in the exact center.

Fig. 16

MAKING WHEELS ON THE DRILL PRESS

Using the Hole Saw

The use of a hole saw, such as the one shown in Figure 16, is an ideal way to make true, round wheels with the axle hole in the exact center. These saws are also available in the hardware sections of department stores and in hardware stores. They usually range in size from ⅝-in. diameter (which is too small for our use) up to and including 4-in. diameter as illustrated. When using the drill press, clamp a piece of the wood to the press to protect it. Run the drill press at its lowest possible speed; the manufacturer of the hole saw recommends that the speed not exceed 200 r.p.m. As a precautionary note, it is best also to clamp the stock in place.

The hole saw has a mandrel that takes a drill which centers the saw on the stock and drills the axle hole. It is best to drill and cut from one side first until the drill comes through the stock, then turn the stock over and complete the sawing. Wheels made in this way need virtually no sanding or finishing.

Single and Two-Wing Wheel Cutters

A single-wing cutter, as shown in Figure 17, is another excellent tool for making wheels in a hurry. The unit consists of a chuck with both a square and round shank. The chuck holds a replaceable ⅛-in. drill that cuts the axle hole. In operation be certain that the drill extends far enough so that it enters the wood before the cutting bit does. The arm holding the cutting bit is adjustable so that holes of any diameter from ⅞ to 4 in. may be cut. Stores carry these cutters in two sizes. Special care should be taken when using a wing cutter, for the bar holding the cutter bit turns rapidly and could strike the fingers sharply if they get in the way. In using a wing cutter, one half of the cutting is done from one side, the stock is turned over, and the finishing cut is made from the opposite side.

Fig. 17

Two-wing cutters, such as those shown in Figure 18, are also available. These cutters operate on the same principle as single-wing cutters except that with two cutters there is better balance in the operation and less chance of binding, especially in thick stock. These cutters usually cut wheels from 2 to 8 in. in diameter. Again, the drill should extend far enough to enter the stock before the cutter bits. These wing cutters may be used in both the drill press and a portable drill but the drill press is better and safer.

Fig. 18

Two-Wing Contour Wheel Cutters

These efficient wheel cutters, as illustrated in Figure 19, have two shaped knives which contour the surface of the wheel into the shape of a tire and wheel hub. The knives are adjustable on the bar so that wheels of various diameters may be made. They also employ a replaceable drill that drills the axle hole. In operation, one side is cut first, the stock is then turned over, and the finishing cut is made from the opposite side. These contour cutters produce excellent wheels similar to those turned on the lathe as shown in Figure 13.

Fig. 19

Other Methods for Making Wheels

There are still other methods for making wheels. For example, the axle holes can be drilled in the rough-cut stock and the pieces threaded on a suitable machine bolt. A nut on the bolt clamps the pieces tightly together. The extending threaded portion of the bolt is then held in a drill press or a portable drill. The drill is started and the pieces are cut to size with a wood rasp or file. This method works but it is not recommended, since some danger is involved.

Commercial Wheels

Many hobby and craft shops carry a complete line of wheels as shown in Figure 20. Rubber wheels from ½ to 3 in. in diameter, various hardwood wheels, plastic spoked wheels, and hardwood spoked wheels up to 6 in. in diameter are available. These are all quality products and they save much time in the construction of toys. However, they do not give the craftsman the satisfaction of making the entire unit by himself.

Fig. 20

Suppliers

Wood and Dowels
Local lumberyard

Scrap Wood
Cabinet shops
Any woodworking shop
Builders and remodelers
Pattern shops (foundries)

Exotic Woods
Constantine & Son, Inc.
2050 Eastchester Road
Bronx, New York 10461
(Catalogue 50¢)

Craftsman Wood Service
2724 Mary Street
Chicago, Illinois 60608
(Catalogue 50¢)

Hardwood
2125 Goodrich Avenue
Austin, Texas 78704
(Catalogue 50¢)

Mosley Company
Route 3, Read Road
Janesville, Wisconsin 53545

Midland Walnut Co.
Box 262
Savannah, Missouri 64485

Tools, Hand and Power
Hardware dealer
Tool section, department store

Hard-to-Find Tools
Brookstone Co.
Brookstone Bldg.
Petersborough, New Hampshire
03458

Nails, Screws, Hardware, Glue
Hardware dealer
Tool section, department store

Finishing Materials
Paint store
Hardware store
Paint section, department store
Hobby shop